THE FOOLISH CORNER

AVOIDING MIND TRAPS IN PERSONAL FINANCIAL DECISIONS

THE FOOLISH CORNER

AVOIDING MIND TRAPS IN PERSONAL FINANCIAL DECISIONS

JOHN HOWE
WITH ROBB CORRIGAN

STUART
CHARLES
GROUP

Published by Stuart Charles Group, Columbia, Missouri

Edited and Designed by Girl Friday Productions
www.girlfridayproductions.com

Editorial: Emilie Sandoz-Voyer
Interior Design: Rachel Christenson
Cover Design: Paul Barrett
Image Credits: cover © ID1974/Shutterstock

ISBN-13: 978-0-9985107-0-5
ISBN-10: 0-9985107-0-X
eISBN: 978-0-9985107-1-2

Library of Congress Control Number: 2016921482

First Edition

Printed in the United States of America

To those who wish to understand themselves better and avoid ending up in a foolish corner

CONTENTS

INTRODUCTION

There is a foolish corner
in the brain of the wisest man.

—Attributed to Aristotle

I have spent the last thirty-five years teaching finance, doing economic research, and serving as a financial consultant. In that time, I've tried to pay attention to what works and what doesn't when it comes to how we humans behave around money. One thing I've noticed that *doesn't* work is people effectively giving away money or other assets when they don't mean to. Why would we do such a foolish thing? It's not in our self-interest, that's for sure. But as psychologists, economists, and others who research human decision making have found time and again, we humans are often exceedingly good at shooting ourselves in the foot when it comes to money. Of course, we are good at other things too—lots of things, more positive things. But financial foot-shooting we are experts in, even though we don't want to be.

I would like for there to be more intact toes in this world: that's why I have written this book. It is intended for readers like you: intelligent and inquisitive people who might have an inkling that when they contemplate designing a retirement strategy for years ahead, or even consider buying a new washing machine next week, there are unseen psychological forces at work that can negatively affect how those decisions play out. Unfortunately, most of us typically become aware of these forces only after the damage is done, if we do at all.

This book, therefore, is for people who want to identify, explore, and then master those forces. This is the book to read *before* opening other books that get into the gritty details about stock investing or 401(k)s and the like.

Just to give you a flavor of what I am talking about, I'll start with a few questions:

- *Do you find that you hate a $100 decline in your savings account more than you love a sudden addition of $100? That's because all of us have a natural tendency toward something called "loss aversion."*
- *Do you tend to "follow the herd" in your financial decision making? No? Not even a bit? Are you sure? I'll explain why no one should believe you!*
- *Do you know how you might be making yourself perpetually unhappy with what you own and your place in the socioeconomic pecking order? I do, and will show you an antidote to that poisonous thinking.*

As you can sense, I will be using some academic vocabulary, but I will make plain exactly what the terms mean. Much of this terminology comes from a fast-growing segment of economics research called "behavioral finance." This fascinating area of study is largely based on the notion that human psychology, with all its emotional peculiarities, has much more to do with our financial decision-making processes than do standard economic models based on purely rational visions of markets and their human agents. Those visions have their value and place, but increasingly we economists are discovering that behind them the more complex human psyche is truly controlling the scene. That's why many of the contributors to behavioral finance are, in fact, psychologists.

Throughout this book I will introduce interesting new research from behavioral finance that helps illuminate dimly lit terrain that could use more light. That said, this book is not intended to be an encyclopedia of behavioral finance, but rather an introduction to some of the more important, practical, and relevant ideas from that field related to financial decision making—with many pertinent lessons included from my years of pondering that topic. Important terms and concepts have been bold-faced or italicized along the way and can be found in a summary at the back for quick reference.

Someone who has done even more pondering than I about this topic is Daniel Kahneman, who is without question the acknowledged godfather of behavioral finance. Now in his eighties, Kahneman is a psychologist who won the Nobel Memorial Prize in Economic Sciences in 2002 for his work on the cognitive biases that all humans share to one degree or another and how they affect our decisions. In 2011, Kahneman published the book *Thinking, Fast and Slow,* which summarizes much of his life's work and went on to become a *New York Times* bestseller.

In his book, Kahneman uses some basic terms that have become accepted as common language among behavioral finance experts, sometimes with slight alterations. For our purposes, the most important of these terms concerns his description of human decisions as arising from two "systems." System 1 is fast, visceral, and largely involuntary. System 2 is more contemplative, reflective, and rational. For example, selling a stock that has dropped in value because of a fear of further loss is System 1 in action. Selling a stock because analysis shows that the company's prospects have changed for the worse is System 2 in action.

The distinction between the two systems is important because System 1 is affected by a larger and more insidious range of mental biases and other cognitive limitations. My approach in this book is, first, to effectively make you aware of how System 1 is influencing your life, and, second, to provide you with the tools for making more decisions with System 2. I will continue to use some of Kahneman's helpful terminology here and there as we go along.

This book will be of value to a wide range of people. For starters, it will be useful to baby boomers and post–baby boomers (Generation Xers), who, as a whole, have not yet saved enough for retirement. Better decisions on their part may mean that they actually have the chance to retire when they want to. Those just starting their careers will be interested too. If they can head off on a good path just out of college, they will lay a solid financial foundation that should serve them well through the inevitable cycles of good and bad economic times. All should be able to learn some tricks within these pages to help keep from stumbling into a foolish corner.

I have been assisted in this undertaking by my longtime friend and onetime doubles partner, Robb Corrigan, who has served primarily as editor of this book but also as a true coconspirator in its development. Robb has followed an unconventional path all his life, having started out studying philosophy, then working as a financial journalist at daily newspapers, and eventually serving as a managing director of one of the world's largest asset-management firms, based in London. He is the "with" on the cover, but he is more than that, and the book would not exist without his efforts.

CHAPTER 1

COMPARED TO WHAT?

Escape from the Hedonic Treadmill

"A friend asked me, 'How's your wife?'" comedian Henny Youngman said in a famous routine. "So I says, 'Compared to what?'"

The response is surprising and amusing, but it contains an important truth: we often judge ourselves (and others) on a relative, not absolute, basis. And for the most part, we are unaware of doing so. In this chapter we'll explore some interesting examples of this phenomenon, show how it can hurt our well-being (financial and otherwise), and describe what we can do to counter this altogether-too-common human tendency. This is a very apt starting point for our exploration of the psyche's pitfalls when it comes to finance and for the pathway to avoiding them.

Many of you will remember the 1980s, or have heard of them. It was an era when the economic dominance of the United States was, to all appearances, eroding dramatically. The country set to knock the United States off its perch was

Japan, an emerging powerhouse that seemed to come out of nowhere. Only a decade or so earlier, "Made in Japan" had been perceived to mean "junk." But by the 1980s Japanese manufacturing was increasingly efficient and produced high-quality products (think of Honda or Sony). Japan's economic reach extended well into US territory itself, as Japanese investors bought such notable properties as New York City's Rockefeller Center and California's famous Pebble Beach golf course. Americans' fear of Japanese economic dominance on the world stage was suddenly evident everywhere.

At the peak of Japanese influence, a pollster asked Americans this question: Which of the following scenarios would you prefer?

Japanese economic growth of 6 percent and American economic growth of 4 percent

OR

Japanese economic growth of 1 percent and American economic growth of 3 percent

What do you think the response was?

The vast majority of respondents in fact preferred the second alternative. But consider for a moment what the second option actually meant. People chose an America that was economically weaker, economically less well-off, just so it could be ahead of Japan. In a word, the respondents to the poll were judging themselves relative to the Japanese, rather than in absolute terms. Clearly, their views were self-destructive, but how many of the respondents truly understood and internalized that? Very few, I suspect.

At a more individual level, we've all heard of "keeping up with the Joneses." The phrase refers to our tendency to compare ourselves with our neighbors or with members of a perceived peer group. When your neighbor Jones gets a new car, your own car begins to look a little shopworn, and the urge to buy a new one grows—or so it is for many people.[1] Then Jones has the gall to put a swimming pool in his backyard, and suddenly you might wonder how you've gotten along all these years without one yourself.

Hence, we encounter a seemingly never-ending cycle of dysfunctional thinking. First, the Joneses might always be ahead of you, at least in your eyes. You can end up feeling like a greyhound chasing a mechanical bunny: you run as fast as you can, but you never quite catch it. So keeping up with the Joneses can mean chasing a target that is always out of reach, and perhaps the gods of personal happiness meant for this to be the case. And even if you do "catch" the Joneses, the Smiths across the street have just bought two new cars and installed a pool themselves—only this one is Olympic-size! Even if you apply merely a tiny amount of your mental bandwidth in this direction, it is remarkably easy to find an unattainable target. For all your life I guarantee that there will be at least one benchmark of this kind that you can't match, or can match but only for a little while at best. In fact, it is many people's default behavior to subconsciously seek out such impossible benchmarks and pursue them. And that's a tragedy.

To make matters worse, the Joneses and the Smiths don't even have to be people in your neighborhood or peer group. In fact, they don't even have to be real. According to researcher Juliet Schor of Boston College, "Television viewing results in an upscaling of desire. And that in turn leads people to buy."[2]

---

1. See, for example, Joshua Shemesh and Fernando Zapatero, "Thou Shalt Not Covet Thy (Suburban) Neighbor's Car" (working paper, University of Southern California).
2. This quote is from CNNMoney.com. The research can be found in Schor's *The Overspent American: Why We Want What We Don't Need* (New York: Harper Perennial, 1999).

Characters in sitcoms, not to mention the manufactured personalities of "reality TV," can have enormous influence via their clothes, possessions, and lifestyles. Schor estimates that every additional hour of TV watching per week boosts spending by approximately $200 a year per viewer. The average American household watches six hours of television a day. If half of that time consists of sitcoms and reality shows, it could cost a household thousands of dollars a year in excessive consumption! Forget about keeping up with the Joneses or the Smiths—now people are struggling to keep up with the likes of the Kardashians.

Closely related to this phenomenon are the somewhat disturbing effects of what behavioral economists call ***hedonic adaptation***. This cognitive bias can be defined as the notion that "changes in income or experiences *temporarily* affect happiness, but as people become accustomed to the new situation, the impact diminishes."[3]

Put differently, hedonic adaptation refers to the idea that the "feel good" aspects of a purchase or an accomplishment fade rather quickly. If you're anything like the rest of us, you've experienced this. When you drive that new car you just bought off the lot, you feel great. The car looks spiffy, you pump up the radio volume a bit, and you are confident—perhaps on a subconscious level—that there will be admiring glances as you drive into your neighborhood or slip into your parking space at work.

But what about six months later? Most of the thrill probably has worn off. The exterior of the car has a few dents, the kids have spilled things and left litter in the back, and the engine doesn't quite get the gas mileage that the salesman promised it would. The honeymoon is definitely over.

---

3. Research by Tim Kasser of Knox College shows that people who place a high value on material goals are unhappier than those who are less materialistic: http://www.slideshare.net/rnja8c/hedonic-adaptation-happiness.

A similar phenomenon is seen with people who come into large amounts of money. Take lottery winners, for example. There is near euphoria at the onset of the windfall, with overwhelming thoughts of all the things that can be bought with that huge wad of cash. Yet studies show that about a year later, lottery winners report they are just as happy as they were before they won the lottery.[4]

So there is an all-too-short period of high satisfaction once some desired object is obtained or a highly sought-after goal is achieved. But sooner or later the feeling fades, and you now turn toward the next acquisition in an effort to regain that feeling. Perhaps a bigger car would make you happier? A larger income? And so you redouble your efforts, working hard for the next new and best thing.

This cycle is referred to as the ***hedonic treadmill***. You run and run, and you run even harder, but you don't seem to get anywhere in terms of psychological well-being. Of course, you may be accumulating material goods, but your finances likely are suffering, and your overall happiness isn't much improved, if at all.

So what can be done about this sad state of affairs? First, let's note that hedonic adaptation can work *for* us when negative events happen in our lives. Hedonic adaptation means that negative events have less of a lasting effect on happiness than we might expect. The most striking evidence of this phenomenon is that paraplegics report happiness levels that are not much lower than the happiness levels of the population at large. They have apparently adjusted to the extreme physical setbacks that they've encountered. Another example, closer to home, is my nineteen-year-old son, who is a type 1 diabetic. He wasn't very happy when first diagnosed, but now, after a

4. Whenever I recount this research, the audience reaction is always "Well, that wouldn't happen to me." But there is every indication that it would.

few years of acclimating himself to the routine of managing his disease, he seems at least as happy as his classmates.

But hedonic adaptation works against us over the long haul as we focus on trying to acquire ever more of the "good things" in life. Typically, we are unaware of this pattern; it is System 1 in action. Let's take a look at how you can get out of this race to nowhere by powering up System 2.

Ideally, you should start by trying not to think of your financial life in relative terms. That is, avoid thinking, "How am I doing relative to the Joneses?" There will always be some hypothetical Joneses somewhere who are doing better than you by some relative measure (income, wealth, good-looking kids, prestige of university degree, exotic vacations, etc.). Rather, try to think in absolute terms: I am healthy; I have food and shelter, a loving partner, and so forth. Good things do exist in your life, and they are often very good things—all on their own.

But given the human tendency to think in relative terms, it is not always possible to avoid relative thinking. If that is the case, how then can we diminish its negative effects? The overall approach to getting the better of this kind of rat race can be inferred from the Henny Youngman quote at the beginning of this chapter. Specifically, when you think about how happy you are in life, how satisfied you are with the way things are, be careful to notice how your mind is operating. If you really wish to consider your life in a compared fashion, quiz yourself: Compared to whom? Compared to what? In short, it is important to consciously choose your comparison group and to understand the implications of that choice. If you compare your net worth to that of Bill Gates, you are always going to be dissatisfied. Unless you are Bill Gates or Warren Buffett or a few others, you will always be much less wealthy than someone. Such a comparison only leads you down the path toward dissatisfaction.

So if you have to choose a comparison group, do so consciously and do so with the intent of increasing your life satisfaction. For example, if your household income is greater than $51,017, it is higher than 50 percent of the households in the United States (based on 2012 US Census data) and higher than at least 95 percent of the households worldwide. As a reader of this book, it is likely that your household income is, or will soon be, higher than $51,017. You are well-off relative to almost everyone in the world!

You can also choose historical comparisons. For example, the lifestyle you lead is almost infinitely easier than the lifestyle of royalty two hundred years ago—modern toilets, reliably potable water, antibiotics, et cetera. None of these existed back then. So in regards to some of the basics of life, you are better off in many ways than almost everyone who has ever lived!

The physicist Stephen Hawking has a neuromuscular disease and is almost completely paralyzed as a result. He communicates by use of a special electronic device. He is wheelchair bound. And yet he has stated that he is grateful for his disability because it has allowed him to focus on his (deep) thinking. He could lament the fact that he can't play golf or go for a walk in the woods or do any number of physical activities, thereby comparing himself to physically able people. But indications are that he avoids such comparisons and focuses on the good in his life.

Another technique for getting off the hedonic treadmill is described by William B. Irvine in his book *A Guide to the Good Life: The Ancient Art of Stoic Joy*.[5] He calls it "negative visualization." To put it briefly, he suggests that you identify something good in your life and then imagine what your life would be like if it were gone. What if your spouse died? What if you lost your health? In a society such as ours that has been

5. New York: Oxford University Press, 2008.

steeped in the power of positive thinking, this approach seems unconventional at best. But Irvine argues that there are two benefits to negative visualization. First, it can act as a sort of "dress rehearsal." If the negative event does occur, you are somewhat prepared to deal with it. Second, and more relevant to our purposes, negative visualization creates more appreciation for what we already have, thereby reducing the urge to jump on the hedonic treadmill.

It is human nature to look at life in relative terms, but how we frame and interpret that comparison is critical to how we feel about ourselves and our situation. So it is vitally important to be aware of when we make these comparisons and, when we do so, to make conscious choices about the comparison group we choose and the goals we set for ourselves.

Without conscious choices, we may discover ourselves on a perpetual hedonic treadmill, always unhappy. And, in fact, we might find that by some comparison-based definition, we've actually managed to win the rat race. The problem then is we're still a rat.

CHAPTER 2

MONEY ILLUSION

A Dilemma: To Eat the Food or the Menu?

Money is money, right? The reassuring face of Benjamin Franklin on a one-hundred-dollar bill somehow feels like a guarantee that a hundred dollars is indeed just that, just what it says—one hundred bucks. But take that same "Benjamin" from a ways back in time, such as 1975, and try to spend it here in 2017. What could you get now? A rough answer: about 17 percent of the goods that you could have bought forty years before. Your hundred bucks has become a pitiful seventeen dollars.

That's scary news. Clearly, something happened over those decades, even though Mr. Franklin's face has remained remarkably unchanged. We are now stumbling into less certain territory, but it is territory that is incredibly important to understand. And our starting point should be the question: "Just what is money anyway? Is it really something hard and unchanging, or is it something else?"

We could start with the physical aspects of money itself, of course. Money has taken many physical forms in the past, such as conch shells, beads, and gold coins, and in modern times it also takes electronic form, including the controversial Bitcoin currency. But it is readily clear that in today's economy, these objects themselves don't really have much value, or almost never the value stated on them. The paper that a buck is printed on is not worth a buck, for example: it's worth less than one cent, in case you wanted to know.

So to truly understand money, we can't refer to its physical characteristics. A more promising path looks toward its function: What does money do? The short answer is that money allows us to buy things (goods and services), both now and in the future. So money is, in some sense, not real. It is, in fact, abstract because it represents the *capacity* to buy things, but it is not the things themselves.

And herein lies a fundamental misperception. Economists call it ***money illusion***. This bias arises when we confuse the physical aspect of money itself with its actual "purchasing power," its capacity to be exchanged for goods and services. Another way economists put it is that money illusion is the confusion of *nominal* value (the face value, or number of dollars stated on the physical piece of paper) with *real* value. And real value is just another way of saying how much "power" you have to purchase specific items. This is the "purchasing power" you sometimes hear economists talk about.

In other words, money illusion is akin to mistaking a menu for the food itself.[6]

Why does this happen? Primarily because people don't properly take inflation into account. Inflation is commonly defined as a rise in the overall prices of goods and services. If a package of gum cost $1.00 a year ago and $1.06 now, there has

6. A paraphrase from Alan Watts's *Does It Matter?: Essays on Man's Relation to Materiality* (New York: Vintage Books, 1971).

been inflation in the price of gum. That's 6 percent inflation, to be precise. Further, if prices have risen for most goods—not just for gum—then we are talking about inflation that applies throughout the economy. Inflation in this wider sense means that the purchasing power of the dollar has declined. Hence, a dollar is no longer enough to buy a package of gum, or a lot of other things that might have been valued at a dollar a year ago.

Now consider how *not* taking inflation into account can lead to money illusion.[7] Suppose that your salary this year is $50,000. Over the ensuing twelve months inflation is 5 percent. Roughly speaking, this means that the goods and services that you purchase have gone up in (nominal) price by 5 percent. Now suppose that at the end of the year you get a 3 percent raise, so you're now making $51,500. On the surface, it might look (and even feel) to you as if you're better off at the end of the year. After all, you're making $1,500 more than you did last year. But if you think this way, you are suffering from money illusion. Why? Because your purchasing power has actually decreased. Prices have risen faster than your salary: you're behind the game, in a very real and painful way. Your new salary can buy fewer goods and services at the now-elevated prices than your year-ago salary could at the old prices.

Is grappling with money illusion important? The answer is yes, for several reasons. Let's start at the big-picture, or macroeconomic, level. Professors George Akerlof and Robert Shiller have argued in their book *Animal Spirits*[8] that a type of money illusion may be responsible for housing bubbles. They explain that people mistake the nominal increase in the value of their house for an increase in real wealth (purchasing power), when in fact it reflects only the decrease in the purchasing power of

7. In an essay in a book that he coedited, Daniel Kahneman provides a similar example: *Choices, Values, and Frames* (Cambridge: Cambridge University Press, 2000).
8. *Animal Spirits: How Human Psychology Drives the Economy, and Why It Matters for Global Capitalism* (Princeton, NJ: Princeton University Press, 2009).

the currency (inflation). Believing that they are truly wealthier, they shift toward less saving and more spending. Even more dangerously, they may borrow against the increased house value, for example, and take out a second mortgage. Should that value decline, as happened in the financial crisis of 2008, they find themselves owing more than the house is worth. At this point, they are forced to spend less. When millions of people do this, the economy can head straight downhill. Consequently, money illusion at the personal level may have been a contributing factor to the dramatic swings in economic cycles that we have recently experienced.[9]

At the microeconomic end of the spectrum, individuals who are subject to money illusion make inferior financial decisions. They think they're getting wealthier when they are not. As described above, money illusion tends to change consumption and savings patterns for the worse. Under its dangerous influence, we consume more and save less than we otherwise would (and should) when prices are rising. With insufficient savings, we run the risk of finding ourselves in old age with the equivalent of a tin cup and a monkey, plus a fistful of nearly worthless currency.

So how do we overcome our money illusion tendencies? First some bad news: there is evidence that the tendency to fall for money illusion is hardwired into our brains.[10] As psychologists put it, dealing with nominal values is "cognitively easier" (or, as the rest of us might put it, "easier"). It's the knee-jerk thinking typical of Kahneman's System 1. So overcoming

---

9. Money illusion may also lead to the mispricing of the stock market (see Franco Modigliani and Richard A. Cohn, "Inflation, Rational Valuation and the Market," *Financial Analysts Journal* 35 [March/April 1979]: 24–44). This too can distort the macroeconomy and exacerbate swings in the economic cycle.
10. Bernd Weber, Antonio Rangel, Matthias Wibral, and Armin Falk, "The Medial Prefrontal Cortex Exhibits Money Illusion," *Proceedings of the National Academy of Science* 106, no. 13 (2009): 5025–28.

money illusion is not going to be easy. But it can be done, and it starts with awareness. Once you are aware of the issue, some straightforward thinking and calculations will serve you well. You will shift your decision making from System 1 to the more rational System 2.

The key to defeating money illusion is to learn to think in real values, not nominal values. In other words, the trick is to think in purchasing power terms—sometimes called "inflation-adjusted values"—not mere face values. Real values reflect true purchasing power, and what is true helps set us free. Let's consider an example.

Way back in 1981, I managed to achieve a lucky escape from graduate school; fortunately, I remained intact for the most part—and with a PhD in hand. At that time, I was driving a positively ancient car and was thinking about buying a new one. The average price of a new car at that time was about $20,000. By 2008, the average new car cost about $36,000.[11] If you knew the inflation rates for each year between 1981 and 2008, you could calculate the inflation-adjusted price of a new car in 2008. You would then have an "apples to apples" comparison that would reflect the real (inflation-adjusted) price of a new car.

This calculation can be a bit tedious. Luckily, there are websites that do this for you, such as http://www.westegg.com/inflation/infl.cgi, which is free. For its calculations, this website uses the government's Consumer Price Index, or CPI—the most widely accepted measure of inflation. The Westegg site shows that, if car prices had risen from 1981 to 2008 at the same rate as the CPI, a new car would have cost $46,800. As noted, it actually cost only $36,000. This means that in inflation-adjusted terms, a new car was cheaper in 2008 than it was in 1981 (contrary to what many people think!). Obviously,

11. Source: http://seekingalpha.com/article/81546-real-prices-for-new-cars-keep-going-down.

of course its nominal price has risen, given that it took more dollars to buy a new car in 2008 than it did in 1981. But relative to the increase in prices of other goods, a new car had actually gotten cheaper! Put differently, in purchasing power terms, a new car cost less in 2008 at $36,000 than it did in 1981 at $20,000.[12] It is worth noting that the calculation does not account for the improvements in quality and safety in new cars over that time period.

This approach to adjusting nominal values using the CPI, or other broad price indexes, is the standard way of adjusting prices at different points in time for inflation, as almost any basic economics textbook will show you. But at the individual level this calculation is precise only if your income has increased at the rate of inflation. By that I mean if your income has increased at the same rate as the CPI from 1981 to the present, then a new car is indeed cheaper today from your perspective than it was in 1981.

An alternative way to think about purchasing power adjustments is to think about *your* purchasing power. Suppose in 1981 you were making five dollars an hour. At that time, you would have needed to work four thousand hours to earn the purchasing power necessary to buy a new car. Suppose that you are now making eight dollars an hour, and a new car costs $36,000. You would have to work almost forty-five hundred hours to earn the purchasing power to buy a new car.[13] In your personal case, the real cost of a new car, relative to your income, has *increased.* This has occurred because your nominal income increased less (in percentage terms) than the increase in the nominal price of a new car. Nominally speaking then, your income went up 60 percent, but the price of a

12. Perhaps counterintuitively, the real prices of many natural resources have actually declined over time; see Charles W. Howe, *Natural Resource Economics: Issues, Analysis, and Policy* (New York: John Wiley & Sons, 1979).

13. Calculated as 36,000 / 8.

new car went up 80 percent. If a similar pattern exists for other goods that you buy, your overall purchasing power has clearly declined over this interval.

I call this concept ***individual purchasing power*** (IPP), a new term that appears for the first time here in this book. It is important because it tells you about the purchasing power of *your* income over time. IPP asks: Is that power going up, down, or staying about the same? It reflects *your* economic reality, not the economic reality based on a broad measure of inflation, for example, the CPI.

Armed with the wisdom gained from understanding IPP, you will make better decisions. For example, you will not be fooled by the increase in your wage from five dollars to eight dollars an hour, thinking that you are automatically getting ahead. Instead, you will recognize that, in personal purchasing power terms, your wage may well have decreased over time. You will make different decisions with this understanding, compared to the decisions you would make if you thought you were always getting a truly higher salary over time.

Up to this point we have (1) talked about the conventional notion of money illusion, and (2) adapted it to a person-specific version (IPP). But there are other forms of money illusion, although they are not usually labeled as such. Let's look at four additional types and their antidotes.

A good place to start is with ***odd-even pricing***. That's the marketing practice of setting a price for a retail product in odd numbers, just under a round even number—for example, $49.95 rather than $50.00, $0.99 rather than $1.00, and so forth. The motivation for odd-even pricing is the hope that consumers' attention is drawn to the *4* (in $49.95), thereby causing them to think of the product as a $40 item, not a $50 item, or something very close to that notion. Although there is surprisingly little rigorous research to support the effectiveness of this pricing strategy, it is used by many retailers (including the giants, such as Walmart). Hence, it's reasonable to assume that it influences at least some consumers' decision making, or else retailers simply wouldn't do it.

The antidote to odd-even pricing is to relearn how to round numbers (you didn't learn everything you need to know in kindergarten—rounding came later). So \$49.95 becomes \$50.00, which is much closer to the actual cost. Being aware of the full price of an item will lead you to make better decisions. You dispel the illusion of a \$40 item when the more accurate assessment that it is a \$50 item comes to the fore.

Another type of money illusion concerns ***pretax pricing*** versus tax-inclusive pricing. In the United States, prices are almost always quoted pretax, with gasoline prices and airfares as notable exceptions. So if a \$49.95 item is subject to a 7 percent sales tax, the total cost is \$53.45. Europe, however, offers an interesting contrast. There, prices are almost always quoted inclusive of taxes.

Is the European way better? Not for US retailers, even if it is for those of us visiting Europe. Research shows that if US retailers post tax-inclusive prices, consumers buy about 8 percent less of the good in question.[14] In a world of perfectly clear thinking, this shouldn't happen. Why? Because the sales tax rate is well known and it is not difficult to calculate what the total cost of the item would be if pretax prices were used. Put differently, the final cost of the good is the same whether tax-inclusive or pretax prices are posted, but consumer demand is significantly different in the two cases. Apparently, consumers subconsciously, and therefore unknowingly, think of the posted price as the final price, even if there is tax to be paid. The illusion is that the posted price is the final, total price.

---

14. Raj Chetty, Adam Looney, and Kory Kroft, "Salience and Taxation: Theory and Evidence," *American Economic Review* 99, no. 4 (September 2009): 1145–77.

The primary antidote to "pretax" thinking is awareness that it is the total expenditure that matters, not the posted price. I suspect that the tendency to "anchor" your thoughts on the pretax price comes from the desire to get a "bargain," and in theory, the lower the stated price, the better the bargain. But knowing the sales tax rate and having at hand a simple calculator—like the one in your smartphone—will allow you to make a better-informed decision.

At this point you might well ask: But isn't this trick of citing the basic price without all the added taxes, fees, et cetera, one of the oldest marketing gimmicks in the world—and one of the most pathetic? I'd have to agree it is. And yet the number of people, educated and otherwise, who fall for it on a daily basis is astounding. (By the way, I think the biggest culprits of this are probably major hotels, with their city, state, occupancy, hospitality, and sales taxes, et cetera, bolted onto the basic price. Retailers and the like are pikers in comparison.)

Let's next consider the case of foreign currency. If you've grown up in the United States, your financial experiences have largely been with US dollars. You develop a sense of what constitutes a high price and what makes for a low price. But when the currency changes, it is difficult to adjust mentally; a ***currency adjustment*** is needed. In effect, you have anchored your expectations about prices to one specific currency. Let's consider the case of the British pound and the US dollar, and let's assume you are a Yank visiting London. As I write, the (post-Brexit-vote) British pound (£) is valued at $1.22. That is, it costs you $1.22 to buy one pound.

Contemplate your jet-lagged mind-set as you walk around London. You see a souvenir that you've always craved, say a shot glass engraved with the image of the Queen making a header in a soccer match. Invaluable art, no doubt. It costs two pounds. It is natural to think of this price as, in fact, two dollars because you have been mentally "anchored" to dollars your whole life. Your basic unit of money has been one dollar, or two dollars, or one hundred dollars, but always dollars. Of course, two British pounds is not two US dollars. The cost is actually $2.44, calculated as 2 x $1.22. But two British pounds can "feel like" two US dollars, especially since, in this case, these two currencies do not have wildly different levels. (For a real disparity try the Japanese yen: one US dollar will get you more than one hundred yen!)

Compounding your difficulties is that if you are not a frequent international traveler, a British pound may not look like "real" money to you. It is hard to avoid the notion that it could be money from a British Monopoly game. When you pull those pounds out of your wallet or purse, it just doesn't seem like you're spending real money.

As with the other types of money illusion, the antidote first consists of awareness of the problem, followed by a straightforward calculation and some clear thinking about the amount you are actually spending. Knowing that the shot glass costs a hefty $2.44 (as mentioned, British prices are tax inclusive), you can now ask yourself: "Is the shot glass worth it?" It might be, but now you are making a much more informed choice.

The last form of money illusion we'll review involves the use of ***credit cards versus cash***. Various claims have been made about how much more people spend when they use a credit card as compared with cash. The range of claims is from 13 percent up to a 100 percent (!) increase in spending per person associated with credit card use.[15] This is because people often don't think of the use of a credit card as being equivalent to spending actual cash. Similar to the case of foreign currency, they don't feel as if the use of a credit card is the same thing as

15. The latter figure comes from http://www.moneycrashers.com/you-spend-more-money-when-you-use-a-credit-card/. This website also notes that credit cards can encourage impulse buying and can lead customers to purchase more expensive merchandise than they otherwise would, outcomes that ultimately result from money illusion.

spending "real" money. This effect is partly related to the fact that the benefits of the spending (e.g., a Big Mac) are realized right away, whereas the pain associated with the spending (the credit card bill) is postponed. But it is also the illusion that the use of a credit card is somehow not the same as spending real money. This illusion can be so strong that at least one financial guru advises people not to have even a single credit card. Although this antidote is extreme, for some people it can be very effective. If you're not willing to go without a credit card, awareness that credit card expenditures are as real as cash expenditures will help dampen the illusion.

Given all this evidence, I hope you realize that money is not truly cold hard cash, fixed and constant, despite what we might consciously or subconsciously believe. It is, in fact, an abstraction. It represents nothing more than the power to purchase, the ability to buy goods and services—and that is an ability forever in flux. Hence, money easily becomes subject to illusions. Just keep in mind this point: while a pretty face like Franklin's remains constant on a one-hundred-dollar bill, that doesn't mean the number next to it is timeless as well.

CHAPTER 3

MYOPIC LOSS AVERSION

Chronic but Curable

Myopic loss aversion, or MLA. Yikes—sounds almost deadly. Well, in a way it is, for your finances at least.

MLA is a behavior pattern, or bias, that in the context of investing causes us to unnecessarily make transactions too often, thereby reducing our net returns. It is widespread among investors of all stripes, and it may even be contagious. The good news is that it is better understood than ever before, thanks to some groundbreaking studies in behavioral finance. There is no perfect antidote yet, but if you recognize the symptoms in yourself and follow the advice below, you might just make a full recovery—and be much healthier in mind and wallet for it.

Before jumping into the specifics of MLA, we need to quickly run through ***prospect theory***—the foundational background to this common affliction. At its core, prospect theory is very simple: it states that investment losses tend to "hurt" us more than investment gains of the same magnitude "please" us. There are many examples and variations of this. One of the simplest examples: losing $1,000 pains us far more than gaining $1,000 makes us happy. More specifically, some research suggests that the pain of a $1,000 loss is equivalent in magnitude to the pleasure of a $2,000 gain.[16] Taking this even further, economist Tyler Cowen states, "The idea of any loss at all matters more than the size of the loss."[17] An extreme view perhaps, but it reflects an intrinsic truth: financial losses—not to mention losses in general—really do hurt!

One of the more recent pieces of evidence for this was the 2008 market plunge and its resulting barrage of media coverage. Many investors simply refused to look at their financial statements. They just didn't want to experience the pain of seeing their assets decline in value yet again, resulting in piles of unopened mail.

Prospect theory can largely be explained via a simple graph of pain and pleasure:

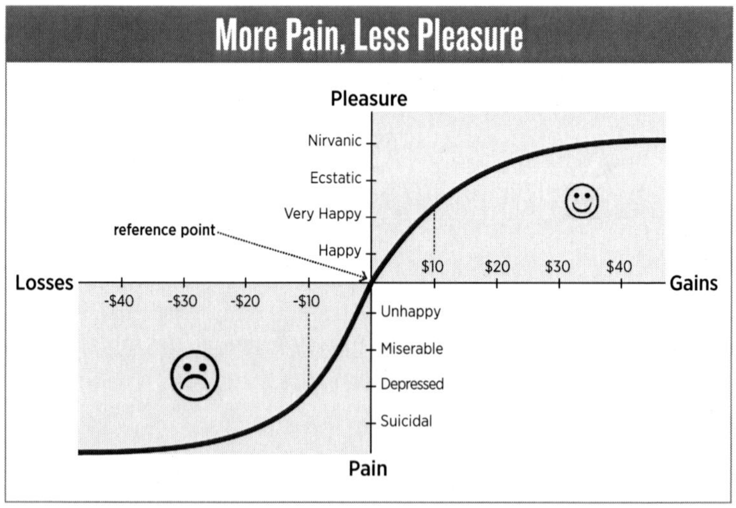

16. Amos Tversky and Daniel Kahneman, "Advances in Prospect Theory: Cumulative Representation of Uncertainty," *Journal of Risk and Uncertainty* 5 (1992): 297–323.
17. "7 Steps to Get Your Finances Back on Track," CNNMoney.com (March 31, 2010).

Think of the "reference point" as being your current level of wealth. If your wealth increases by ten dollars, you feel better off—you are in fact "quite happy." But what happens if you lose ten dollars instead? Obviously, you feel worse off. But prospect theory says that you feel much worse off with the ten-dollar loss than you would feel better with the ten-dollar gain. Although the two potential payoffs are symmetric (+/– ten dollars), your feeling about them is not. As we say in the economics game, your feeling is actually "asymmetric." That is, it's unequal and unbalanced.

As mentioned in the introduction, psychologist Daniel Kahneman received the Nobel Prize in Economics in 2002 in part for his work on prospect theory. Many other academics in recent years have built on this fine work, meaning that we have increasing evidence that the vast majority of human beings are subject to this psychological phenomenon. What compounds matters is that people then act on the feelings that prospect theory describes, and that behavior is MLA.

The primary symptom of MLA, within the context of investing, concerns how frequently we view our investments' performance. Matters then take a sharp turn for the worse when we decide to take some action on those investments as a result of looking at their performance too much. Why do we do this? In part because we have forgotten some of the basic premises of investing.

One of those premises, in the understated words of legendary financier J. P. Morgan, is that "stocks will fluctuate." A simple point, but how true. In fact, all but the safest investments exhibit some level of fluctuation, or as it is more commonly called on Wall Street, volatility. What is crucial to know is that even though there has been some dramatic volatility in this century, leading to severe plunges, the prices of even quite risky assets have trended upward over time.

Hence, if we were to look at our investment portfolios less frequently, we would be more likely to see gains than losses. Consider an extreme case: a financial Rip Van Winkle, someone who doesn't view his investment portfolio for twenty years. Because of the long-term upward trend in prices, it is almost certain that, over any twenty-year interval, Rip will find his portfolio is worth more when he wakes up than it was when he went to sleep.

But if we look at our portfolios frequently, we are more likely to see losses, simply because prices jiggle around a lot in the short run. We are "sampling," or observing, our portfolio more frequently and seeing the fluctuations around the long-term upward trend. We are shaking in our boots because we see all these "losses" as a result of our nervous "sampling."

Here's another example. There are about 250 trading days on the stock market in a year. Suppose that a good investment goes up on 135 of these days and down on 115 days, which is enough to generate a typical upward trend and a nice return on your money for the year. If we observe our portfolio every day, we do see more winning days (135) than losing ones (115). But prospect theory states that the losses, even though they are really just "paper" losses because you haven't sold your stock yet, hurt more than the gains are enjoyed. So viewing our portfolios frequently, for example, daily, is likely to leave us feeling worse off than we would if we looked only occasionally—say, quarterly.

And how do we react to feeling worse? As humans, we tend to avoid things that encourage us to feel bad. If we associate feeling bad with our investments, we tend to take action to reduce that pain—and in the case of capital markets investing, that means selling the stock creating the pain. This behavior is myopic because it occurs even when we have good investments, ones that in the longer run are trending up in price. That's where we get the word *myopic* in myopic loss aversion.

A bad case of MLA results in selling perfectly good stocks and other investments at the wrong time, thereby unnecessarily realizing losses while incurring transaction costs along the way—a double whammy.

How do we combat MLA? My advice: make informed and wise investment decisions, within the context of a long-term strategy—then don't look at your investments too often. What does "too often" mean in practice? Unfortunately, there is no clear-cut answer. Daily is clearly too frequent. And, of course, more than once a day is too frequent as well. So unless you are a professional trader, turn off the running tickers on your computer screen! Some financial advisors suggest that you examine your investments quarterly, coincident with quarterly financial information received from financial institutions. This is reasonable advice.

In addition, when you do examine your investments, you should resolve to wait for a time after seeing the results (say, a day) before taking any action in response. This waiting period gives a chance for System 1's immediate and emotional reaction to die down and allows you time to think more rationally about what you are going to do—that is, use System 2. You may have heard advice along the lines of "Before making a big purchase, wait a day or two. You could discover you really don't need or want it." The same advice applies to financial decisions, both buying and selling.

And note that observing your portfolio quarterly doesn't mean that you should trade it that frequently. For an average investor, a yearly interval between trading is probably more appropriate. To see why, let us start with the distinction between portfolio rebalancing and market timing.

Portfolio rebalancing is trading designed to return your portfolio to its original target asset allocation, or mix of investments. For example, you may decide that your optimal stock/bond mix is 60 percent / 40 percent. If over the course of, say, a year, stocks outperform bonds, you might well end up with a 70/30 mix. That's a very normal and frequent occurrence. Rebalancing would involve selling some stocks to return to your original strategic mix of 60/40.

Portfolio rebalancing has nothing to do with timing the market—that is, trying to overweight your portfolio with stocks when they are undervalued and underweighting it when stocks are overvalued. Portfolio rebalancing is merely a mechanical adjustment back to the target stock/bond mix, with no assumptions about whether stocks or bonds are the better investment. I am a fan of portfolio rebalancing. I am not a fan of market timing, given that an extensive number of studies suggest that few, if any, investors can successfully time the market.

How often should you rebalance? There is a happy medium to be struck between having a portfolio that has drifted from your target allocation on the one hand, and the transaction costs associated with rebalancing (which include bid-ask spreads, commissions, and taxes) on the other. While no absolutely definitive, general answer can be given, my recommendation is that you rebalance once a year. In general, you could justify rebalancing more often when markets are volatile (because you are likely to drift further away from your target allocation). Conversely, in smooth markets that are moving "sideways," you might choose to rebalance less frequently than once a year.

In short, examine your portfolio occasionally and rebalance infrequently. Preferably do so via a strategy that you have thought out and predetermined, and that you intend to stick with. By doing all that, you will free a good chunk of your mental bandwidth to concentrate on activities that are much more likely to generate income for you and your family: specifically, whatever you are trained to do and what you do best, relative to other people. That is the strongest preventive medicine I know for staying out of the MLA intensive care unit.

CHAPTER 4

THE RANDOMNESS TRAP

Musings on Patterns

Have you ever lounged on the grass on a balmy summer's day, looked up at the sky, and seen the image of Lady Gaga somewhere in the billowy clouds? If not her, what about a laughing hyena? George Washington? Scooby-Doo? If so, congratulations: you're good at ***pattern recognition***!

Let's try to put that skill to a more practical use. The chart on the next page shows the stock price of global conglomerate John Galt & Co. over the past decade. Do the data points seem random, or can you perceive something more interesting? A double-peaked mountain? A gulch, perhaps? A declining trend with regular spikes upward?

If you do, you are like many people who have observed this chart and seen patterns in the form of continuations, reversals, or seemingly predictable undulations. You might also identify other regularities. For example, in some cases (not necessarily in the chart following), it might seem that after a stock has gone down two days in a row, it goes up on the third day.

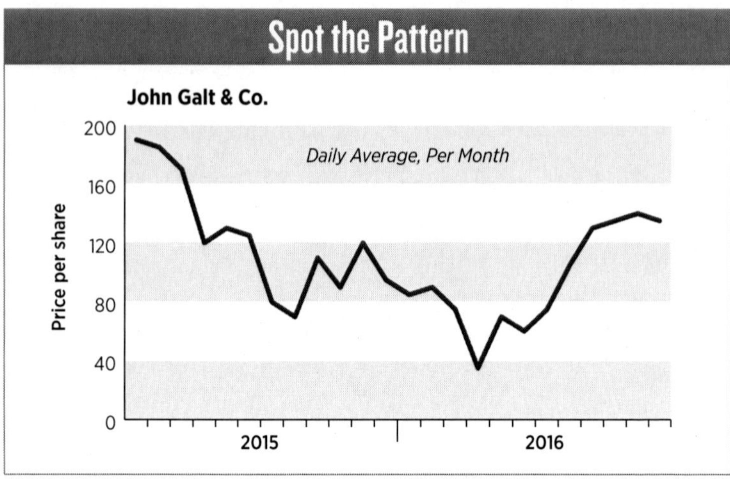

Source: FlowPrice Inc.

The art of trying to predict the future of a stock's price from its historical price chart is called "charting" or "technical analysis."[18] There is a lot of jargon in this game, but the notion here is simple: with sufficient and careful analysis, the charts will reveal a pattern of some sort. By "pattern," chartists mean a recurring regularity in the behavior of the price. The price may bounce up off a "support level" or bounce down from a "resistance level." Occasionally there may be a "breakout," suggesting that the stock is off and running in a clear direction, either up or down. A chartist might also examine a stock price graph and decide that it has "calendar regularities"—for example, a stock that rises in price every January, or every third Friday of the month. All of these are supposed patterns that typical chartists believe are the key to predicting future stock movements,

18. The terminology surrounding technical analysis is used differently by different authors. *Charting* may refer to patterns in prices only, whereas technical analysis might also consider changes in trading volume and the use of many other indicators. This chapter focuses on price charts, but the arguments against charting, when used by average investors, carry over to many of the more extensive systems of technical analysis.

giving them a huge leg up on other investors who don't try to identify such patterns.

Now it is confession time. The chart above of "John Galt & Co." stock is not an actual stock price chart. Instead, I created it by choosing at random the price changes from six possible outcomes: +20 percent, +10 percent, +5 percent, no change, −10 percent, and −20 percent, each with equal probability. The initial price was pegged at $200, and the price changes were then just added on. Imagine that each price change you see has been determined by a roll of a (fair) die with these six outcomes on its faces. There can be no regularity or predictability from such a process, because each roll of the die is independent—what happened on the last roll has nothing to say about what happens on the next. Yet this process generated the seemingly nonrandom price chart you see, complete with a "pattern" or two at least.

Sorry about the deception. But I think it was very handy in driving home this important point: what looks like a pattern in a set of data often is not.

Forty years ago, Burton Malkiel, an economist at Princeton University, showed a randomly generated price chart similar to the one above to a professional technical analyst who specialized in stocks. Malkiel's chart was a simple creation, similar to mine for John Galt & Co.: he flipped a coin, and if it came up heads, he showed that as a price increase; if it came up tails, he showed that as a price decrease of the same magnitude. As described in Malkiel's classic book *A Random Walk Down Wall Street,* the technical analyst got quite excited when he saw the resulting chart, and begged to know the name of the stock; after all, it was about to break out on the upside! "We've got to buy immediately. . . . There's no question the stock will be up 15 points next week."[19] Malkiel notes drily, "He did not respond

19. Burton G. Malkiel, *A Random Walk Down Wall Street* (New York: W. W. Norton & Company, revised college edition, 1975).

kindly to me when I told him the chart had been produced by flipping a coin. Chartists have no sense of humor."

Of course, just because people see patterns that aren't there doesn't mean that there are no patterns to be seen. Since Malkiel first conducted his price chart experiment, there has been research that shows some patterns exist in stock returns. I summarize this research at the end of this chapter. But I also argue there that the few patterns that actually do exist are not in fact exploitable for anyone but a small handful of professional investors (and even for them, great time and effort are required); therefore, this notion is best left alone by the vast majority of investors.

In truth, humans naturally seek out patterns and trends because this ability has been honed by evolution. A pattern-detecting bias is virtually embedded in our genes, and it has been key to our survival. For example, there are many cycles in nature, ones that are regular and often predictable. The person who could know the pattern of the seasons with some level of certainty was better able to predict when migrating herds would pass nearby, allowing him to take advantage of this knowledge. As agriculture developed, the person who identified the seasons accurately was better able to time the planting of crops. Thus, people with the ability to detect patterns were more likely to survive, reproduce, and pass along that skill to their offspring. It is clearly a human trait to look for patterns and regularities, and it may have saved us as a species. The trick, though, for modern humans is to figure out when we are observing patterns that are real and when we are interpreting nonpatterns as patterns.

While I hope I have now offered enough evidence to win over even the most hard-core believers in pattern chasing, or at least make them wobble a bit, I offer yet another example for any remaining naysayers—this one from the world of sports. Consider, if you will, the topic of shooting success in basketball.

Basketball coaches, players, and fans almost universally believe in an intriguing phenomenon they call the ***hot hand***. A player who is fortunate enough to have a hot hand will have made several of his previous shots, indicating to hot-hand believers that he is more likely to make the next one—compared to a situation in which he has missed several previous shots.

The concept of the hot hand looks straightforward, but it has a crucial subtlety: *more likely than what* to make his next shot? Shooting a basketball is not like flipping a coin—a player has a long-term success ratio that may exceed 50 percent or be less than 50 percent. In contrast, the probability of heads coming up (analogous to the player making a shot) is a fifty-fifty proposition.

So having a hot hand implies that the probability of the player's next shot going in is *more likely* than his long-term average success rate. That is, if there is such a thing as a hot hand, knowing that he has made several previous shots means that we can predict a "higher than normal" probability of him making the next shot.

As I mentioned, belief in the hot hand is widespread. For example, coaches often leave the last critical shot of a game to the player with the apparent hot hand. Commentators often think in the same way. However, researchers have searched extensively for evidence of a hot hand, and it cannot be found.[20] Indeed, a string of successes—say, five three-pointers in a row—actually seems to be followed by a slightly *lower*-than-normal probability of making the next shot! You might be thinking that this is caused by more defensive pressure applied after a series of shots made, but the result holds for free throws as well, a setting in which there is no defensive pressure (though there

---

20. Thomas Gilovich, Robert Vallone, and Amos Tversky, "The Hot Hand in Basketball: On the Misperception of Random Sequences," *Cognitive Psychology* 17, no. 3 (July 1985): 295–314.

may be other kinds). The rather stunning conclusion must be this: the hot hand is a pattern that isn't.

Now let us turn our attention back to financial markets. In a comprehensive article by three New Zealand professors,[21] the authors examine the profitability of more than five thousand "trading rules"—that is, rules usually based on technical analysis and patterns that stock traders could use to help them succeed in the markets. The study focused on how the rules performed in markets in the forty-nine countries included within the widely followed and respected Morgan Stanley Capital Index. The researchers conclude that technical analysis does not add value "beyond that which may be explained by chance." That is, there were some trading rules that were profitable, but their frequency can be explained by random chance. In effect, this is a variation of the old Texas saying that "even a blind squirrel finds an acorn now and then." The important point is that because such findings occur by chance, a seemingly profitable trading rule based on patterns is unlikely to continue to make money consistently—even for the professional traders who can somehow identify such patterns.

This effect is perhaps best summed up by an insightful comment by Nassim Nicholas Taleb, one of the world's foremost experts on patterns and randomness in financial markets. In his bestselling book *Fooled by Randomness*,[22] Taleb concludes: "Markets are a mere special case of randomness traps." And who wants to be caught in a trap?[23]

---

21. Ben R. Marshall, Rochester H. Cahan, and Jared M. Cahan, "Technical Analysis Around the World" (working paper, Massey University, New Zealand, 2010).
22. *Fooled by Randomness: The Hidden Role of Chance in Life and in the Markets* (New York: Texere, 2001).
23. And I will add that Daniel Kahneman (you know the name by now) writes, "My views on [the role of chance] have been influenced by Nassim Taleb" (*Thinking, Fast and Slow,* p. 14).

So how do we overcome our inbred tendency to see patterns even when they do not exist? Again, awareness is key: be on the lookout for when your explanation of an investment's success, or when someone else's explanation of theirs, seems to be based on a pattern. And keep in mind that the bias toward trying to parse out patterns is primarily a System 1 activity—inborn and intuitive. That makes it an activity that is generally unhelpful for financial decision making.

I used to believe that people trained in the natural sciences or engineering were particularly susceptible to believing in patterns in financial prices, precisely because they are trained to find them in nature. (And in these scientific fields, pattern recognition often can be extremely helpful and, in fact, critical.) But recently my nineteen-year-old son, who has a modest stock portfolio and no engineering training, clicked on the graph of a stock and remarked, "It looks like it is doing well. I think I'll buy it." He saw a pattern of "good performance," and therefore thought it would likely continue.

The belief in patterns is deeply ingrained in human nature, apparently at an early age. Clearly, I have some fatherly work cut out for me.

Hunting for Momentum—Best Left to Professionals (with Very Deep Pockets)

I admit it: changes in prices are not quite without patterns. Specifically, there is evidence of "momentum," in stock prices at least. As the word suggests, *momentum* refers to the empirical regularity that well-performing stocks tend to continue to perform well. For example, a study[24] made a few years ago shows

24. Elroy Dimson, Paul Marsh, and Mike Staunton, "Momentum in the Stock Market," chapter 3 in RBS / ABN AMRO *Global Investment Returns Yearbook*, February 2008.

that the twenty stocks that performed best during a defined twelve-month period substantially outperformed a portfolio consisting of the twenty worst performers over the following year. Hence, momentum is certainly a pattern, isn't it?

Yes, at times. The studies of momentum at least account for a number of things, including rebalancing costs, the risk of the securities selected, and the potential that the findings are attributable to chance. None of the possible effects fully offset the apparent profits to be had from momentum investing. However, one of the authors of the study does note: "To exploit momentum, you need investors who understand the portfolio is going to be subject to a very high level of volatility." As an article in the *Economist* goes on to say, "Trend-followers can get 'whipsawed' in volatile markets, buying at the top of a short-term trend and then selling at a loss shortly afterwards."[25]

And there is another risk involved in the momentum strategy: in the longer term, periods of high returns are followed by periods of low returns (another type of pattern called "long-term reversal"). Thus, when trying to exploit the momentum effect, you have to know when to sell. And that can be very difficult. In short, momentum is a type of pattern, but it is not clear (1) that individual investors can actually exploit the pattern successfully on any consistent basis, or (2) that the significant amount of time and training needed to come anywhere close to doing so is at all worth it, unless professional trading is your profession. And even if you are a pro, it is difficult to make money following this approach over time.

25. "Why Newton Was Wrong," the *Economist*, January 6, 2011.

CHAPTER 5

HERD ON THE STREET—AND IN THE OFFICE

How to Control Your Inner Lemming

The crowd, as a crowd, performs acts that many of its members, as individuals, would never be guilty of. Its average intelligence is very low; it is inflammatory, vicious, almost simian.

—H. L. Mencken, Damn! A Book of Calumny *(New York: Philip Goodman Company, 1918)*

I now bravely move on to the topic of ***herd behavior***, the tendency for us humans to be swayed by an often infuriating but extremely influential force: "the crowd." Sometimes this influence is quite obvious, as when our drinking buddies successfully urge us to down one more beer. But sometimes it is rather subtle, frequently acting at the subconscious level—even in the world of finance and investments. For example, in lemming-like fashion we might pile into tech stocks, buying near the top of the market, and suffering when the (next) bubble pops. Or we might pick up on cues we get from others—and late-night infomercials—and decide to speculate in real estate, only to be sucked down by a big decline in prices. Following the crowd can be extremely dangerous, especially in the wrong place at the wrong time. A vision comes to mind of the actor Graham Chapman shouting to a crowd in the Monty Python movie *Life of Brian*: "You must learn to think for yourselves!"[26]

Before digging into the dangers of following the herd, I will note that there are times when crowds are useful.[27] For example, if you are trying to estimate the number of jelly beans in a jar, the average guess of a large number of people is likely to be more accurate than an individual guess. A similar argument applies to the stock market. The notion is that share prices are often right about where they should be, reflecting a collective viewpoint about the safety or riskiness of a company's stock. In fact, the stock market taken as a whole can be viewed as closely akin to one of the many new tricks of our digital age: "crowdsourcing." That is, using the Internet and social media networks to put questions in front of thousands if not millions of eyeballs in the hopes of getting some useful responses, or of getting a handle on what a large number of people think about a certain topic.

But in far too many situations, following the crowd leads to bad decisions for individuals, especially in the financial world—where the results often have been so disastrous. This herd behavior occurs for four related reasons. First, large numbers of investors have common sources of information. For example, a piece of news about a company and the resulting effect on its stock hits the Bloomberg News service, and

26. After which the crowd responds in unison, "We must learn to think for ourselves!"—not quite getting the point.
27. An excellent book on this topic is *The Wisdom of Crowds* by James Surowiecki (New York: Anchor Books, 2005).

thousands of people become aware of the details. To the extent that the meaning of this news is clear (bad news, for example), investors will react the same way to it: a common behavioral response to commonly shared information. The herd then dumps a particular stock because the news is deemed to be bad.

A second reason for herd behavior is social norms. It can be palpably uncomfortable to stand out from the crowd. This is especially true in certain cultures—for example, closely knit societies found in Japan and Korea—though the culture of Wall Street as a whole also suffers significantly from this affliction. In many cases it may be considered impolite—or downright career threatening—to question the tacit assumptions of a group. One magazine writer tells the story of questioning the investment strategy of an investment club: "I might as well have told the . . . Baptists that they should also consider that Buddha fellow. . . . I felt uncomfortable."[28] Being the lone voice can be painful and awkward, not to mention professionally destructive.

The third reason for herd behavior is what behavioral psychologists call the ***affect bias***. This refers to the notion that our unconscious perceptions about products or investments are based on emotional responses to the asset in question, including superficial aspects of the asset. Such responses about companies, for example, can be influenced by a company name alone. A *Financial Times* article notes the positive effect of the name "YUM! Brands"[29] on consumers' decisions to purchase its products. During the Internet bubble in the early 2000s, a firm that changed its name to include ".com" enjoyed a near automatic bump up in its stock price, even when there was no change in the fundamental business of the company.

---

28. Robert Frick, "Don't Trust the Crowd," *Kiplinger's Personal Finance*, December 2009.
29. Rodney Sullivan, "The Role of the Subconscious in Market Behaviour," *Financial Times* (July 14, 2011).

This occurred because many people perceived the change to be positive and subsequently acted in concert. They bought as many "dot-com" stocks as they could get ahold of, not consciously considering that they were part of a herd headed in a bad direction. And that herd galloped merrily onward, straight over a cliff.

A fourth reason for herd behavior is "group think," the well-researched tendency of individuals within a group to converge on a common view. Experiments have shown that people can be convinced by their confederates that one of two line segments of equal length is longer than the other. This curiosity holds true despite the fact that the reality of the situation is clearly the exact opposite. Many experiments of this type have been performed, confirming this basic result. Recent evidence suggests that these results are not simply the person being bullied into giving an incorrect answer. Using brain scans, researchers have shown that the subject's actual perception is changed via the persuasion of others.[30]

Further, group think continues to pop up everywhere, even after it has been studied and written about for decades. For example, one recent study shows that the drinking habits of college students are strongly influenced by their perception of other students' drinking habits, especially ones that were excessive.[31] But in a sober moment, which we hope is most of the time, do college students truly wish to be mindlessly swayed in this manner? Probably not.

---

30. Gregory S. Berns, Jonathan Chappelow, Caroline F. Zink, Giuseppe Pagnoni, Megan E. Martin-Skurski, and Jim Richards, "Neurobiological Correlates of Social Conformity and Independence During Mental Rotation, *Biological Psychiatry* 58 (2005): 245–53.
31. Maria T. Moreira, Lesley A. Smith, Nerissa Santimano, and David R. Foxcroft, "Social Norms Interventions to Reduce Alcohol Misuse in University or College Students," *Cochrane Database of Systematic Reviews*, no. 3 (July 8, 2009).

Another example is investment clubs, at which peer pressure is particularly strong and investment performance often poor. Such results at these clubs generally have been attributed to group think.[32] At the corporate level, there is evidence that when banks make decisions to foreclose on individual homeowners, as well as businesses, their actions are taken in a "contagious" manner, meaning another form of herding.[33]

But, you may say to yourself, I don't invest via an investment club or similar "crowd." I sit at my desk by myself, or alone in my study at home, making calm decisions unaffected by whatever popular sentiments may be swirling outside. Surely I'm not subject to group think, right? Very likely you are completely wrong. As with the drinking habits of college students, you are influenced by your *perceptions* of what others think and what others are doing. So, for example, you might interpret high volume in a stock that has recently risen in price as evidence that others have a positive impression of the stock. And you don't have to consciously think that: there is evidence that behaviors such as smoking and overeating, not to mention our moods, are significantly contagious at the subconscious level.[34] Just because you are not directly in contact with others acting in a certain way does not mean you are not subject to herd mentality!

And the news is no better (indeed, worse) if you log on to Internet chat rooms or discussion boards for investment ideas. A chat room is a classic setting for herd behavior. Consider, for example, a study of RagingBull.com, a popular Internet

32. Brad M. Barber and Terrance Odean, "Too Many Cooks Spoil the Profits: Investment Club Performance," *Financial Analysts Journal* (January/February 2000).
33. Ryan Goodstein, Paul E. Hanouna, Carlos D. Ramirez, and Christof W. Stahel, "Are Foreclosures Contagious?" (working paper in economics, no. 11-12, George Mason University).
34. Tyler Cowen, "In-Your-Face Consumption Is So 2007," CNNMoney.com, April 7, 2009.

message board. A study by New York University professors[35] shows that on days with abnormally high message activity, trading volumes are correspondingly high. However, the volumes are not predictive of stock returns. The authors conclude that the comments posted on the message board are "noise," not useful information. But investors react in concert to the posts, creating a herd effect.[36]

Hang on a second. Certainly, high-end finance professionals can rise above group think, right? Especially given their education, training, and general high level of intelligence? After all, the incentives are very strong to "get things right" within the rarified world of investment banks and professional trading floors. Unfortunately, the news here is no more encouraging. There is a substantial body of research that documents extensive herding by a wide variety of financial market professionals. Their frequent crowding together in a pack around similar strategies and investments is widely known.

So what can we do to avoid being negatively influenced by the crowd? As with all the human biases and frailties discussed in this book, the first step is awareness—in this case knowing that the bias exists, not just in others but also in you. Your awareness slows down the engagement of System 1. By reading this far into the chapter, you've already come a good way toward accomplishing that. The next step is to be aware of specific times when you might be subject to herding influences. This is tougher still and requires System 2 to kick in. The examination of one's own motivations and emotional state within

---

35. Robert Tumarkin and Robert F. Whitelaw, "News or Noise? Internet Postings and Stock Prices," *Financial Analysts Journal* 57, no. 3 (May/June 2001): 41–51.
36. There is evidence of similar influences over consumer purchases. For example, buyers of apps for Facebook are influenced by the purchasing decisions of others. See Jukka-Pekka Onnela and Felix Reed-Tsochas, "Spontaneous Emergence of Social Influence in Online Systems," *PNAS* 107, no. 43 (October 26, 2010).

fluid situations is often difficult and sometimes uncomfortable. But the rewards can be substantial, if you end up avoiding making purchases of certain stocks near the top of an Internet bubble, for example. So here are some pointers that will allow you to steer clear of inadvertently joining a financial herd.

First, feeling somewhat smug about a financial decision or strategy because "everyone is doing it" or even because "a lot of people I respect" are doing it should raise a red flag in your mind. Do you remember your mother ever saying to you, "Well, if everyone jumped off a cliff, would you do it too?" When we are in financial lemming mode, that's exactly what we do. A common setting for "everyone is doing it" is the apocryphal cocktail party, especially one that is populated by your respected peers or "socially acceptable" neighbors. "What, you don't own any [insert current fad industry here] stocks? My broker says they can't miss." Your alarm bells should be going off at this point, in a very loud fashion. As noted earlier, it can feel uneasy to go against conventional wisdom. That's the price you have to pay, though, to truly escape these kinds of behavioral traps.

Second, and conversely, feeling uncomfortable about an investment or financial strategy can be a positive indicator. It may mean that you are not running with the herd, that you are not allowing your decisions to be influenced by those of others. For many financial decisions, not doing what the herd is doing is a good thing.

I'm not saying everything that feels comfortable is bad or everything that feels uncomfortable is good. But you can use these feelings as triggers to reexamine and reflect on the decisions you are making.

Another antidote to herding is to listen to widely varying points of view—bulls and bears, optimists and pessimists, conservatives and liberals—and then synthesize the information for yourself. As the Monty Python sentiment implies, researching and analyzing opportunities yourself often is the best way forward, time-consuming as it may appear to be. And if you lack confidence to pull this off or don't have the time to do so, then that's quite human. I'll let you in on a secret: confidence, at least of a certain kind, isn't all it's cracked up to be.

A classic study by Philip Tetlock[37] looked at the forecasts of economic and political activity by experts and also asked them how confident they were about their forecasts. The surprising result? The more confident the forecaster was, the *less* accurate were his predictions! So a lack of confidence might even be a sign you are on the right track. Take pride in being a contrarian! And certainly don't rely on the (over)confident "talking heads" that populate the financial airwaves. You can learn a few things from them about investing at times, but do realize that in the end their excessive bravado is primarily noisy entertainment with little useful content.

Finally, let me suggest that you find a devil's advocate to help you challenge your thinking. The concept of the devil's advocate comes from the Catholic Church and dates back to 1587 (the practice was abandoned in 1983). When someone was being considered for canonization, after already having been declared a saint, the church would appoint an advocate to argue against this. The purpose was to ensure that there were no substantial reasons why the person should not be canonized and to make the best possible decision. Like modern lawyers, the devil's advocate did not have to believe the arguments that he was putting forth. Instead, his responsibility was to argue as persuasively as he could against canonization.

Your personal devil's advocate is someone who will challenge your thinking, your logic, and your decisions. It can

37. "How Accurate Are Your Pet Pundits?": http://www.project-syndicate.org/commentary/tetlock1/English. An interesting book on the topic is *Future Babble: Why Expert Predictions Fail—and Why We Believe Them Anyway* by Dan Gardner (Toronto: McClelland & Stewart Ltd., 2010).

be a friend, a spouse, or even someone you don't like—often they are the most honest about the possible silliness of your ideas. Consider, for example, that you are thinking about buying a house. Interest rates are low and prices are down—what could go wrong? Your devil's advocate might say, "Well, housing prices could fall further, you could lose your job, and drug dealers might move into your neighborhood. And you're doing it because everyone in the office is doing it." This would force you to more carefully examine the pros and cons of your decision. Once you have done so, you will make a more informed choice.

If you can't somehow find a personal devil's advocate, you'll have to be one yourself. Many people begin by drawing up a list of pros and cons ahead of making a decision. That's a good start, but you'll need to go further, given that the devil's advocate's mind-set is to bring focus to the cons—something we might not do otherwise. Your devil's advocate, if he is doing a good job, will reduce the chances that what you want to do is being influenced by herd mentality—while increasing the chances that you won't end up in a furry mess at the bottom of a canyon.

CHAPTER 6

CHEERY-O'S—OPTIMISM AND OVERCONFIDENCE

When Are They Hindrances and When Not?

My mum's so pessimistic, that if there was an Olympics for pessimism . . . she wouldn't fancy her chances.

—Nish Kumar, the Edinburgh Festival Fringe, 2012

Have you ever admired the rock-sure confidence displayed by the financial "talking heads" seen on popular business TV shows? They so often seem completely certain that their take on the future path of interest rates, currencies, and the stock market will be 100 percent correct. Such exuberant confidence surely is a key factor in success, in general, and investing, in particular—wouldn't you agree? Consider the subtitle of a fairly typical book on this subject: *The Confidence Factor—Cosmic*

Gooses Lay Golden Eggs by Judith Briles.[38] Most of us would like to have at least a few golden eggs, after all.

Well, for starters a golden (nest) egg would be great, but a focus on exhibiting what is commonly described as confidence may not be the right path to amassing your personal financial empire. Why? Because it is so easy to become *over*confident. And ***overconfidence*** is highly dysfunctional, leading to inaccuracies, distortions, and costly mistakes. As mentioned in the previous chapter, research shows that the *more* confident a political forecaster is, the *less* accurate his forecasts.[39] So it is preferable to avoid being talking-head confident. In addition to bad forecasting, there are other downsides to an excess of confidence, which I will discuss as well. As it turns out, a moderate dose of humility is usually a healthy thing.

And what about overconfidence's (apparent) cousin, ***optimism***? Are there times when you would like to be more optimistic than you are? Rather than focusing on negatives, if you incline that way, would you like to see the glass as half-full?[40] Well, here the story is different—in most circumstances, research shows that optimism is both psychologically and financially good for you (I'll discuss the exceptions).

Before jumping into the details, let's ask, "What's the difference between optimism and overconfidence?" It's a good question because these words are often confused and used interchangeably. But they are different. Optimism is outward-looking, focused on the external world (as opposed to an individual's internal world). It refers to biases and beliefs about exogenous events, events that are not under the control of the

38. *The Confidence Factor* (Aurora, CO: Mile High Press, 2008).
39. Further research from Tetlock: *Expert Political Judgment: How Good Is It? How Can We Know?* (Princeton, NJ: Princeton University Press, 2005). He also notes that the gap between accuracy and confidence is not related to intelligence.
40. Just to be fair to a pessimist, I acknowledge that he will respond in this fashion: "Whether the glass is half-empty or half-full, it is still half-empty."

individual: for example, the weather, financial markets, your children, and so forth.

In contrast, confidence has to do with one's beliefs in one's own abilities, an inward-looking orientation. Accordingly, it often can vacillate wildly, depending on a variety of personality factors.

As discussed later in this chapter, evidence clearly shows that overconfidence is the dominant mind-set of human beings. Put simply, overconfidence refers to *positively biased* beliefs about one's abilities. If you are overconfident, you think you know more than you do and you believe that you can control—or at least influence—events that you cannot. Put another way, overconfident people have a disproportionately positive view of their abilities, in complete disregard of any objective evidence that might be available.

But let's get back to optimism for a moment. Generally, optimism is good for you. For example, optimists on average live longer, are healthier, have stronger immune systems, and persevere more.[41] Entrepreneurs are typically optimists, and their impressive displays of perseverance permit them to deal with the inevitable setbacks associated with starting and growing a company. Indeed, even über-skeptic Daniel Kahneman describes optimism as "the engine of capitalism."[42] Successful long-term investors are often optimists for the same reason: they look beyond short-term poor performance to the longer run, where they fully intend to bask amid broad uplit sunlands. Indeed, in almost all areas of life, optimism is associated with success—however defined.

Interestingly, survey evidence shows that people just about everywhere are, on average, fairly optimistic. In 2008, at the

---

41. See Elaine Fox, *Rainy Brain, Sunny Brain: How to Retrain Your Brain to Overcome Pessimism and Achieve a More Positive Outlook* (New York: Basic Books, 2012).
42. That's the title of chapter 24 in his book, *Thinking, Fast and Slow.*

height of the last financial crisis, 71 percent of Americans believed that the economy would soon improve. Certainly, Americans are known as an optimistic lot, but this trait is true of most nationalities to one degree or another. The pervasiveness of optimism suggests the presence of an evolutionary element. Optimism keeps us looking at the long run and helps us fight through short-term setbacks—obviously good for survival in prehistoric as well as present times.

The bad news about optimism is that some people are not well-disposed toward it, with Nish Kumar's mother (as noted at the beginning of this chapter) as a prime example. Further, people seem to have a "set level" for optimism, and for some, it is set pretty low. The good news about optimism (and hence, reason to be optimistic) is that the set point for that level can be moved up significantly. For specific techniques to lift your optimism level, I refer you to Martin Seligman's excellent book *Learned Optimism: How to Change Your Mind and Your Life.*[43]

So is there any downside to optimism? The answer is yes. When the consequences of being optimistic and yet wrong are severe, optimism might not serve you well. In *Learned Optimism,* Seligman gives the example of a pilot who is optimistic that the wings of his aircraft won't ice up, and thus forgoes deicing. Here, an inclination to pessimism is warranted, especially given the life-and-death aspect of getting such a situation wrong. In the financial realm, optimism about the future returns on your retirement portfolio could also have dire consequences. For example, if you think stocks are going to earn an average return of 15 percent a year—very high by historical standards and thus unlikely to actually occur—you will undersave, have to retire later than planned, or perhaps have to marry for money. Thank goodness you bought this book!

---

43. New York: Pocket Books, 1998.

Interestingly, pessimists tend to be more realistic. So perhaps you want a financial advisor who is a pessimist, even if he isn't a barrel of laughs during your investment strategy sessions. If you are starting up a new business, perhaps a pessimistic business partner could be quite useful—a Chief Pessimism Officer? In building an effective organization, recognize the value of the views of pessimists. As Kahneman and a colleague note, "Organizations actively discourage pessimism [and] when pessimistic opinions are suppressed . . . an organization's ability to think critically is undermined."[44] I'm not recommending that you be a pessimist, only that you value the input of pessimists or, at the least, pessimistic viewpoints.

The bottom line here is that there are numerous benefits to being an optimist and that you can, and probably should, move your optimism set point higher. But be aware of situations in which optimism does not serve you well.

Let's now turn to overconfidence itself. Unlike optimism, there's little to recommend overconfidence. Of course, confidence calibrated to one's actual, empirically verifiable abilities is appropriate. And indeed, you may know quite a few people who are underconfident; such people are not likely to get all that they want out of life. Some degree of confidence, and the implicit self-promotion that accompanies that territory, is helpful in achieving one's goals.

But reaching beyond that into the realm of overconfidence spells trouble, and the evidence suggests we are more likely to be overconfident than underconfident. Robert Shiller, whom we discussed in chapter 2, suggests that "some basic tendency toward overconfidence appears to be a robust human character trait: the bias is definitely toward overconfidence rather

---

44. Dan Lovallo and Daniel Kahneman, "Delusions of Success: How Optimism Undermines Executives' Decisions," *Harvard Business Review* (July 2003): 60.

than underconfidence."[45] And as we'll see, overconfidence is an especially male trait. I'll leave it to evolutionary psychologists to explain that one.

Driving is a near-perfect human activity with which to prove that overconfidence is rampant, not to mention dangerous. Consider this: 80 percent of drivers believe their driving skills to be above average.[46] While good drivers undeniably exist, only about half of them at most can be above average—simply by definition of the word *average*! In short, at least about 30 percent of drivers consider themselves to be better drivers than they actually are. This overconfidence almost certainly leads to increased recklessness, endangering the driver and others. Young male drivers in particular are overconfident and twice as likely as young female drivers to be involved in an accident.[47]

In the realm of corporate finance and CEO decision making, research shows that overconfidence plays a similarly destructive role. How do we know which CEOs are overconfident? After all, overconfidence cannot be easily measured. Some researchers use the number of magazine articles about a CEO as a proxy, with the notion that more articles—in part induced by the PR team—lead to overconfidence. More recently, research has examined the choice of language in CEO communications or the CEO's tone of voice in conference calls to infer overconfidence. Using these indicators, studies show that overconfident CEOs make a wide variety of decisions that serve their companies and their shareholders poorly, especially

---

45. Robert J. Shiller, *Irrational Exuberance* (Princeton, NJ: Princeton University Press, 2000), 142.
46. Ola Svenson, "Are We All Less Risky and More Skillful Than Our Fellow Drivers?" *Acta Psychologica* 47, no. 2 (1981): 143–48.
47. Donna Easterlowe, "'It's All About Trust': Exploring Young (Male) Drivers' (and Passengers')Attitudes to Road Safety": http://slideplayer.com/slide /778067/.

in strategic activities such as their company acquiring another company and paying too much for the privilege.

Richard Roll, a finance professor at Caltech, calls the tendency to overestimate one's abilities and thus to overpay for a corporate acquisition the "hubris hypothesis."[48] *Hubris* refers to an excess of pride or arrogance, a great word to describe overconfidence and to throw around at cocktail parties. I regard Roll's article as one of the earliest examples of behavioral finance research. A hubristic CEO believes that he can manage any company he might acquire with stunning efficiency, forcing "synergies" to be created between his firm and the acquired one—thereby increasing shareholder wealth. Perhaps not surprisingly, research shows otherwise: from a shareholder perspective, it is generally better to be bought out than to do the buying.[49]

In the realm of personal finance, overconfidence has equally adverse consequences. The first of these is the tendency to underestimate risk, possibly because the overconfident investor feels that he can "get out in time" to avoid the risk if he needs to. Alternatively, an overconfident investor might believe that his perception of low risk is calibrated to the correct level, while believing that other investors incorrectly perceive high risk. Obviously, underestimating risk is not beneficial to your investment performance: if you do not grasp the risk you are taking, you set yourself up for greater-than-expected losses in your investments.

A second consequence of overconfidence is the tendency to trade too often. Overconfident investors believe they are

---

48. Richard Roll, "The Hubris Hypothesis of Corporate Takeovers," *Journal of Business* 59, no. 2, part 1 (April 1986): 197–216.
49. An interesting organization that aims to reduce the amount of hubris in the world is the Daedalus Trust (http://www.daedalustrust.com/). This UK-based group hopes to help "rein in reckless leaders," particularly in business and finance. One of its recent position papers is titled "Should Hubris Be a Disease?"

readily able to identify stocks that are both over- and undervalued, and that they can then successfully trade frequently in an effort to exploit the apparent mispricing that results. But this is illusory: they believe they can spot mispriced stocks, but almost always they cannot (recall our discussion of the futility of market timing in chapter 3). And while excess trading might seem benign, every trade is accompanied by transaction costs—for example, broker commissions, bid-ask spreads, and potential tax consequences. The costs of frequent trading can substantially degrade investment performance.

Such costs can be seen in the differential investment performance of men versus women. As noted earlier, men are on average more overconfident than women. When researchers examined the individual trading accounts of investors, they found: (1) men traded much more frequently than women, and (2) as a result, men's investment performance was worse than women's, on a risk-adjusted basis.[50] A 2011 study concludes "that women were more likely to make money in the market, mostly because they didn't take as many risks. They bought and held. Women trade this way because they aren't as confident—or perhaps as overconfident—as men."[51]

So what to do? How can one cultivate optimism and reduce overconfidence, thus dwelling consistently in the sweet spot of "appropriately confident"? Here are some suggestions. First, work to increase your optimism using techniques found in *Learned Optimism* and elsewhere. But remain aware of situations in which optimism might not be helpful to you—for example, in estimating the future returns on your retirement

---

50. Women are, on average, more risk averse than men, consistent with them being less overconfident and thus less likely to underestimate risk. See Brad Barber and Terrance Odean, "Boys Will Be Boys: Gender, Overconfidence, and Common Stock Investment," *Quarterly Journal of Economics* (February 2001).
51. Source: http://www.marketwatch.com/story/women-are-better-investors-and-heres-why-2011-06-14.

portfolio. Being slightly pessimistic (some might say "cautious") will reduce the number of ugly surprises and increase the number of pleasant ones in your financial life. "Nice—I've got more money accumulated for retirement than I expected."

Second, identify and reduce any overconfidence that may be affecting your thinking and behavior, especially if you are male. Start by challenging your beliefs, considering alternative explanations and scenarios, and asking others for a different perspective (see devil's advocate, chapter 5). A popular columnist suggests, "Once you recognize the futility of . . . seeing into the future, your tendency toward overconfidence will diminish."[52] This view may be too extreme, as some features of the future are fairly predictable. But there is clearly value in asking, "What if my predictions are wrong? What is an alternative explanation for what is happening? What if things unfold quite differently than I expect?" These questions help shift your decision making from System 1 to System 2.

To all of this I would add: be humble and agnostic about what you think you know. Writing about the scientific method, Mark Henderson, former science editor at the *Times* (of London), comments:

> [Science] is a way of thinking, the best approach devised yet (if still an imperfect one) for discovering progressively better approximations of how things really are. . . . Science is provisional, always open to revision in light of new evidence. . . . And it is comfortable with uncertainty.[53]

---

52. Bob Frick, "Improve Your Investing Decisions by Ignoring Short-Term Predictions," *Kiplinger's Personal Finance* (November 30, 2011).
53. Mark Henderson, "Science's Methods Aren't Just for Science," in *This Will Make You Smarter: New Scientific Concepts to Improve Your Thinking*, ed. John Brockman (New York: Harper Perennial, 2012).

There are several important ideas for us in this quote. The first of these is the notion that we typically deal with *approximations* of how things really are, not how things really are. Our senses are bombarded thousands of times per minute with all kinds of information. To avoid being overwhelmed, our minds block out a majority of sensory input, so we perceive only a small portion of the available information about reality. Our image of the world is a working model, but not the world itself. That model can be very close to the world itself, or in the case of the overconfident, not.

Another idea in Henderson's quote is that knowledge is *provisional* and is thus subject to being improved upon at any time. For many years, people thought Newtonian physics was the last word in describing the movement of physical objects. Then quantum physics came along. It turns out that movement at very small scales is not well described by Newton's equations. Newtonian physics does work as a good approximation at large scales, but it certainly was not the last word.

Because we deal with approximations of reality and because knowledge is provisional, *uncertainty is omnipresent.* We need to get comfortable with this idea. I'm not saying that you should feel comfortable when dealing with uncertainty, only with the idea that there are very few certainties in life. A realistic attitude about the degree of uncertainty in the world, and therefore our relative impotence at knowing the future, will serve you well in all aspects of your lives, including the financial arena.

As a parting comment, let me remind you to be aware of possible negative interactions between optimism and overconfidence. Consider the pilot who is optimistic that the plane's wings won't ice up. Now add overconfidence: "Even if they do ice up, I can land this aircraft." That's asking for trouble. A finance analogy is being optimistic about future investment returns without considering the alternatives, coupled with a greater-than-justified belief in your financial abilities. That's asking for a hard landing too.

CHAPTER 7

TYING YOURSELF TO THE MAST

Behavioral Aspects of Saving for Retirement

I hope I don't have to convince you of the importance of saving for retirement. But in case I do, I would like to emphasize the single most important aspect of this topic, completely wacky as it may sound: actually saving.

Many people give lots of attention to how their savings are invested. We discussed that in chapter 3. But as long as you are not putting all of your savings in high-risk investments, like lottery tickets or beachfront property in the Sahara, it is the actual act of saving money that is critical. If you wish, you can see this for yourself using any of the retirement calculators available on the Internet. You'll find that improving your rate of return from, say, 5 to 6 percent improves the outcome, but not as much as increasing your ***level of savings***, even modestly.

So saving is important. OK, you've got that. But if you are like many people, you have a ***sense of inadequacy*** in this arena of your financial life. In turn, the discomfort you feel leads you to push the retirement-saving question out of your head. "I'll focus on that when the kids are out of college" is a common thought. Or even more wishfully: "I'll live in retirement on the money I inherit from my parents." Are you sure that they like you that much?

In an era when the funding of government social programs is suspect, saving for retirement has never been more important. Yet survey after survey shows that most people have woefully inadequate retirement assets. According to one, "the average American has saved less than 7% of his desired retirement nest egg. . . . Respondents aged 50 to 59 have saved an average of only $29,000 for retirement."[54]

The situation is actually worse than that: most companies that have pension programs, in the United States and many countries around the world, have moved from generous "defined benefit" retirement plans to stingy "defined contribution" plans. As the name suggests, a defined benefit plan pays retirement income that is defined—typically—by your salary and the number of years you worked at your company. For example, a defined benefit plan might pay an annual retirement benefit equal to 2.2 percent of average salary times the number of years worked. In this setting, your retirement income is fairly predictable and more or less guaranteed.[55] This plan was a pretty good deal for millions of workers for many decades.

In contrast, a defined contribution plan focuses on the contributions of the employer and employee to a retirement account. The amount of money available at retirement then depends on the investment performance of the retirement

54. "Middle Class Falls Short on Retirement Funds," Money, *Reuters*, December 8, 2010, http://www.reuters.com/article/2010/12/08/us-wellsfargo-retirement-idUSTRE6B710K20101208.

55. Since the financial crisis of 2008–9, some defined benefit plans have reduced payouts from their promised levels.

account. In short, the investment risk of a defined contribution plan is borne by the employee, not the employer.[56]

Is this a naughty trick on the part of employers? Many argue that it is. Regardless, though, this new world of retirement saving means increased risk for the uninitiated.

You likely feel uneasy reading all this. You may feel that you are caught in a behavioral whirlpool: first you feel bad about not saving for retirement, which leads you to avoid thinking about saving for retirement, which in turn leads you to think even less about saving for retirement (if that is possible), and little saving for retirement actually happens. A spiral downward, to be sure.

But you need to face up to reality and create a realistic, implementable plan for saving for retirement, and that's what this chapter is all about. A realistic plan will minimize the dysfunctional aspects of human behavior and use insights from behavioral economics to your advantage. Here I will share specific behavioral changes that will put you on the path to sufficient retirement savings.

I'd like us to start by thinking about saving. To state the obvious, saving happens only when you spend less than you make.[57] Put another way, saving happens only when there is deferred gratification, a sacrifice today for a gain in the future. Easy to say but hard to do, as low saving rates attest. Why is this so hard? As with many behavioral traits, this one can probably be traced to evolution. For most of the time that humans have existed, survival has been difficult and life expectancy low. After all, if the saber-toothed tiger eats you today, tomorrow

---

56. For a detailed description of defined benefit and defined contribution plans, see my paper, "Defined Benefit and Defined Contribution Plans," available for free at the Show-Me Institute website: http://www.showmeinstitute.org/.
57. One behavioral weakness is to think of your gross income as "what I make." But you cannot spend or save money that the government has taken; therefore, savings must come from your net income, which is after-tax income.

doesn't matter. In the harsh world of fifty thousand years ago, human energies were focused on day-to-day survival and less thought was given to a hypothetical future.

If you are reading this book, almost certainly you are not living at a survival level. However, our brains haven't evolved to catch up with the new reality. We still tend to take the short view: we can call this ***evolutionary myopia***.

The notion that there is a genetic component to our saving myopia is suggested by the famous "marshmallow experiments."[58] A young child is put in a room with a plate that has a marshmallow on it. The researcher tells the child that if he can wait to eat the marshmallow until the researcher returns (about fifteen minutes later), he can have an extra marshmallow as a reward. Not surprisingly, some children eat it right away, some are able to wait awhile before succumbing to temptation, and a few are able to wait until the return of the researcher.

The children are then tracked over time. The ones with a greater ability to defer gratification also experience much better life outcomes—for example, higher incomes, longer life spans, less obesity, more education, and so forth. This is evidence that there is an inherent genetic tendency for (or against) self-discipline.

But genetics does not explain everything. We can choose to work against our ingrained, inherited tendencies. In what follows, I'm going to offer you some tips for increasing your retirement savings, tips that will enable you to leave that marshmallow on the plate. If you follow these tips, you are using System 2 thinking to prevent System 1 thinking from ever kicking in.

---

58. Walter Mischel, Ebbe B. Ebbesen, and Antonette Raskoff Zeiss, "Cognitive and Attentional Mechanisms in Delay of Gratification," *Journal of Personality and Social Psychology* 21, no. 2 (1972): 204–18.

Payroll Deduction for Savings

This idea is simple and extensively used: have your employer take out a certain amount from each paycheck and direct it to a savings or investment account. Although the idea is not new, our understanding of why it works is new. Remember the graph in chapter 3 that maps out pain and pleasure in regards to myopic loss aversion? Think of your take-home pay as the reference point in that graph. If you do not have savings withheld, then putting some aside by yourself feels like a loss: you bring home one hundred dollars and then put aside ten dollars; in this case, you feel like you have lost that ten dollars, which isn't rational, but real. Remember that the fundamental idea behind MLA and prospect theory is that losses are felt more keenly than gains, so it is difficult for you to set aside money once you have any amount of control over it.

But if your employer has already set money aside for you, there is little or no sense of loss. That is, the ninety-dollar paycheck lands on your desk, the saving already has been done, and the amount of the paycheck is the reference point. Hence, the tried-and-true system of employer withholding has a strong grounding in behavioral economics and is an effective tool for retirement saving. (Self-employed people have the challenge of automating saving in the absence of a separate employer.)

Start Retirement Savings Early in Life

This idea is not new either. It is usually discussed in the context of compound interest. Money invested early has many years to grow, making "interest on the interest" over a long period of time. For example, if you start saving $1,000 a month when you are thirty years old and earn a 5 percent annual return, you will have $1,536,000 when you are seventy years old, ignoring taxes. If you wish to achieve this same goal but postpone the start of your saving until age forty-five, you will have to save $2,580 per month. So compound interest is a perfectly valid reason to start saving early.

But there also is a behavioral issue here. Many of us unconsciously mimic the financial habits of our parents (not to mention other habits). And your parents were influenced by the times in which they grew up. Historically, many people have accumulated the majority of their retirement assets in a relatively short period of time just prior to retirement. This approach is sometimes represented as follows, with the x-axis showing years spent in the workforce, not age, and the y-axis showing amount of money saved:

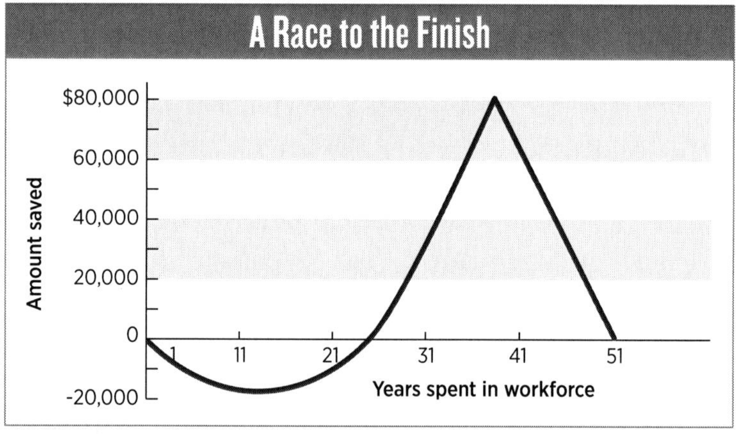

Source: Eugene F. Fama and Merton H. Miller[59]

In this scenario, you don't even cross into positive territory until your twenty-fifth year in the workforce! Although this approach may have worked in the past, it is less likely to work today for at least one reason: many people are having children

59. Eugene F. Fama and Merton H. Miller, *The Theory of Finance* (Oak Brook, IL: Dryden Press, 1972), 49. Available at http://faculty.chicagobooth.edu/eugene.fama/research/.

later in life. So by the time the kids are out of college, there is not time for the "sprint to the finish," as it is sometimes called. To achieve the same $1,536,000 goal by age sixty-five starting at age fifty-five, your monthly saving would have to be $9,890! The risk of this strategy is heightened by the decrease in job security in today's economy.

Worse, the subconscious influence over our retirement decisions need not be limited to our parents. Recall from chapter 1 that, consciously or not, we pick reference groups or individuals against whom we compare ourselves. So, for example, if the characters in our favorite TV shows appear to be living only for the moment (not saving), we might adopt a similar mind-set. The antidote to this subtle but powerful influence is the same as that discussed in chapter 1: consciously and deliberately choose to whom you compare yourself. As documented in the book *The Millionaire Next Door*,[60] a typical US millionaire lives in a modest house and drives a modest car—not the kind of person we see on a flashy reality TV show!

The Save More Tomorrow Plan

The SMT plan is very simple: you commit *today* to increasing your future saving out of *future* salary increases. For example, you might sign an agreement with your employer to deduct from your paycheck 30 percent of all future salary increases. Research shows that most people who were offered the opportunity to enroll in a program providing such an agreement did so and that more than two-thirds of those participating stuck with the plan for at least three pay raises. Perhaps more impressively, savings rates rose from 3.5 percent to almost 12 percent over a period of only twenty-eight months for SMT

---

60. Thomas J. Stanley and William D. Danko, *The Millionaire Next Door: The Surprising Secrets of America's Wealthy* (Atlanta: Longstreet Press, 1996).

participants.[61] One of the behavioral reasons that the plan is effective is that the commitment to future action does not feel like a loss in the present.

If your employer does not offer the SMT plan, ask for it. (It might help if you mention that Professor Kahneman, a Nobel Prize winner, describes SMT as a "brilliant innovation"[62]). In the meantime, you can use a "public commitment" site such as www.stickk.com. There you enter a "commitment contract" with a stated goal. It is not necessary, but if you wish, you can impose a monetary penalty on yourself for failing to meet your stated goal (e.g., a saving target, either in dollar or percentage terms).

Research shows that a commitment contract is very effective in helping people achieve their goals.[63] I'd like to suggest to you that if you choose this approach, the monetary fine go to a cause that you don't like. For example, a Democrat might pledge to pay her fine to the Republican Party—that should keep the motivation high! A less effective, but still somewhat effective, commitment mechanism is a public declaration to your friends or family. Commitments kept secret are the least effective. Did you at least share your New Year's resolutions with someone?

---

61. The original research is by Richard H. Thaler and Shlomo Benartzi, "Save More Tomorrow: Using Behavioral Economics to Increase Employee Saving" (working paper, August 2001). A good discussion of the SMT plan can be found in Thaler and Cass Sunstein's *Nudge: Improving Decisions About Health, Wealth, and Happiness* (New York: Penguin Books, 2009).
62. *Thinking, Fast and Slow,* p. 414.
63. For a good summary, see Gharad Bryan, Dean Karlan, and Scott Nelson, "Commitment Contracts" (working paper, October 2009).

Think About Saving for Others

Many people find motivation in thinking about the good that can be done with financial resources for other people. You might wish to leave your children a significant inheritance, for example. Or you might wish to fund a favorite cause, such as an environmental group. This gives you a specific goal, which increases your motivation to save.

Think About Saving for Your Future Self

I've already mentioned the Save More Tomorrow plan. Another approach is to think about giving your "future self" a gift, the gift of financial security. You might even have a conversation with your future self in which your future self thanks your present self for accumulating wealth. Thinking about your future self gives you a specific reason—and hence, greater motivation—for saving. A specific goal for your future self will add to your motivation: "I'm saving so that my future self will have $1 million in investable assets at age sixty-five." As any motivational speaker will tell you, the more specific the goal, the better.

Here's another way to connect to your future self: "age-progression" software. This software takes a picture of you and "ages" the image. You can look at yourself at your desired retirement age. Research shows that a person who has seen an image of his future self will increase his retirement saving. In one study, students shown elderly versions of themselves reported that they would double their saving![64] An example of age-progression software can be found at http://faceretirement.merrilledge.com/.

64. Jason Zweig, "Meet 'Future You.' Like What You See?" *Wall Street Journal*, March 26, 2011.

Reframe the Consequences of Spending

Some of the earliest research in behavioral economics was on how a problem is presented, or "framed," and on the effects of that framing concerning how people respond to the problem. The classic example of ***framing*** is an experiment in which people are asked about allowing the use of a new drug, using two different frames. The first frame states how many lives the new drug will save, while the second states how many will not be saved by the drug (i.e., will die). Although the information is exactly the same (number saved + number who die = the total), people presented with the first alternative are much more enthusiastic about allowing use of the new drug.

If framing is important, then reframing can be a powerful tool as well. Let me suggest two ways to reframe the cost of spending. If you believe that spending is costly, you will spend less and thus save more. The first reframing to consider is this: How many hours do I have to work to pay for this purchase? Consider the purchase of a $30,000 car. Let's assume you make $90,000 a year. At first blush, it might seem that you have to work one-third of a year (four months) to pay for the car. But note that you pay after-tax dollars for the car, so it could easily be that you need to work half a year to pay for the car. Are you willing to trade six months of your life for the car? Perhaps not. This technique even works for smaller purchases. Do you want to work forty hours for a new TV set, or is your current one good enough?

The second reframing technique is to recognize that money you spend today could be invested; that is, it has an opportunity cost (see p. 81). Now think about the future value of the investment that could have been made. You are giving that up by spending today. Warren Buffett has been quoted as saying, "Do I really want to pay $300,000 for this haircut?"[65] Admittedly, this was either a very expensive haircut or there was a long time for the investment to grow, but I think you get the point. He was thinking about the substantial future sum that someone would be forgoing by spending a seemingly small amount in the present.

Pay in Cash

As discussed in chapter 2, credit card spending can feel like it's not "real" spending. Paying in cash hurts more, so you spend less.

By way of summary, the question you need to confront about your saving behavior is, which Homer do you want to be? It is hard to imagine that Homer Simpson has any money saved for retirement. But the Homer of Greek literature, through the story of Odysseus, shows the benefit of recognizing one's limitations and acting to counter those limitations. Knowing that he could not resist the temptation of the Sirens' call, Odysseus had his crew tie him to the mast of the ship while they passed through to safety. In the same way, you can commit yourself in a variety of ways to saving, in spite of the Siren call of spending.

A Few Thoughts About Retirement Spending

The typical rules that financial planners and others apply to retirement spending are often too rigid. Consider first the question of how much you need to save to retire in comfort. A frequent answer from the planners is that you'll need enough to produce 80 percent of your preretirement income. Let me

65. Jason Zweig, "How Huge Returns Mess with Your Mind," *Wall Street Journal*, January 4, 2013.

suggest that the answer is more nuanced. Depending on your circumstances, spending in retirement could well increase initially; for example, perhaps you and your spouse immediately take trips across the globe that you had been planning for many years. But once that is out of your system, and perhaps with a nudge from a gammy knee or bad hip, you minimize your traveling—as do many seniors. Later, though, depending on your individual health profile, you might need to fork out significant funds for health-care costs not covered by your insurance or Medicare.

My point here is a simple one: a rigid rule such as "80 percent" is, at best, a crude estimate of one's retirement spending needs. People differ greatly in how they plan to spend their retirement years. You need to think about your own individual case and plan accordingly.

Now, consider rules for spending down your retirement savings. There are dozens of them. One of the most prominent today is the "4 percent" rule: you can spend 4 percent of your retirement savings in the first year of retirement and then increase that amount each year to reflect inflation. Simulations show that you are unlikely to run out of money before you die if you use this rule.

The weakness of this rule is that it also is too inflexible. It does not allow you to react to new information that arrives over time. For example, if you think your retirement funds are going to earn a low rate of return over the future, you might use a 3 percent rule. If you discover that your life expectancy is shorter than you had previously imagined, you might use a 6 percent rule.

Thus, the downside to rules is their rigidity. However, too much flexibility is also a bad thing, as our behavioral biases can harm us. For example, people often react to a decline in the stock market by selling all their stocks. Visceral, emotional reactions do not lead to good decisions much of the time in life, especially when it comes to long-term financial health.

So you need a balance—a Goldilocks "just right" amount of flexibility—via a system that allows you to adjust to events that have occurred, but one that minimizes the impact of your emotional side. One way to find this balance is to consider your investment and spending strategies on a regular basis, say, once a year. This approach helps keep you from reacting emotionally but does allow periodic adjustments to your spending habits. And it helps keep you well tied to the mast, even in the most tempting of times.

CHAPTER 8

THINKING THAT WILL WEIGH YOU DOWN

The "Sunk Cost" Fallacy and Other Costly Mistakes

If you have ever taken a basic economics class, you might have the impression that economists are obsessed with costs: total cost, average cost, average total cost, variable cost, and so on. And if you remember those ideas, you might also remember them as tedious and boring. Know why? They often are! Even so, to round out our understanding of behavioral finance, we need to focus on a few types of costs. Understanding them will help you overcome the behavioral biases that I've talked about in the previous chapters. Don't worry: I've narrowed down the list to a tolerable three.

Sunk Costs

Probably the most important cost from a behavioral standpoint is this one. A ***sunk cost*** is an expense that has already been incurred and cannot be retrieved or refunded in any way. For example, if you have bought a ticket to a football game and are not allowed to resell it, the money you spent on that ticket is sunk. Clearly, the money is gone the minute you spent it, as if it has sunk to the bottom of the ocean and will be there forever. The qualification "not allowed to resell it" is important here. If you could sell it for what you paid for it, none of the ticket price would be sunk. If you could resell it for half of what you paid for it, half of the expense is a sunk cost. When I use the phrase *sunk cost*, I'm referring to that part of the expense that is genuinely irretrievable. It may be the full expense or just a fraction of it.

Why are sunk costs important to thinking about financial and other matters? Answer: from a purely logical (but not emotional) point of view, a sunk cost should in no way influence any decisions we make now or in the future. The irretrievability of a sunk cost means that it is irrelevant to decision making from the point of expenditure onward. Returning to the football ticket example, if its cost is sunk, your ownership of the ticket should not influence whether you go to the game. Going to the game will not allow you to reclaim the money: it is gone, whether you go or not.

This conclusion, which sounds reasonable to most economists, sounds rather unreasonable to many noneconomists. "I've spent the money, so I feel that I should go" is a common reaction. The primary reason that people feel that way is they are trying to minimize any regret they might have about the decision. However, it is important to recognize that going to the game (presumably) seemed like a good decision at the time the ticket was purchased. Somehow later, and for whatever reason, it may not seem like that at all. Hindsight is twenty-twenty, but you shouldn't use hindsight to judge your initial decision. That's a bit akin to saying, "I should have bought stocks that went up and avoided those that went down." A truism, but not very helpful. A friend of mine used to say, "If pigs had wings, they'd be pigeons." Also likely true, but of little use.

So how should you think about whether to go to the game? Let's start with a simple case. Needless to say, you will need some System 2 thinking here. On game day suppose it is cold and rainy outside, and you're coming down with a nasty cold. Is it in your best interest to attend? Almost certainly not. What if it is cold and rainy, but you are healthy? Well, that's probably a harder decision. It depends on your desire to see the game and your tolerance of cold and rainy weather. Your call. What if it is a beautiful day, you're feeling great, and it promises to be an exciting game? Then you are likely to go and enjoy the experience. In this context, the decision to go certainly makes sense.

But notice that your decision does not depend on the money you spent on the ticket (I'm assuming its full cost is sunk: there are no refunds available). It is irrelevant to your decision, as it should be. The behavioral part of this story is the regret that you might feel about "wasting" the money. But it was wasted at the time you bought the ticket (although you only know that after the fact). Ancient history, we might say. The regret, like many of our behavioral instincts, is understandable but not rational and can lead us astray.

Let's consider an example from personal investing. Suppose, caught up in the excitement of the property boom of the mid-2000s, you had bought a house as an investment, perhaps to rent out. The real estate market was soaring, your friends were getting rich (or so they claimed), and you didn't want to get left behind. And real estate prices always go up, right? Certainly seemed like a sound investment at the time (remember chapter 5 offered us many tips about avoiding herd mentality).

Then the financial crisis hit in 2008: the value of your property plummeted like a stone, and you were deciding whether to sell it. Recognize that at this point, some—but not all—of your initial investment is a sunk cost. The loss you've incurred doesn't have anything to say about whether to continue as a real estate baron (slumlord?). Instead, you should ask yourself questions that you wish you'd asked earlier: Is real estate management a strength of mine? How does real estate fit into my portfolio? How much risk can I afford to take, and how much risk do I have the appetite to take? Are there demographic or geographic trends that will influence the future value of the property? These questions are not easy to ask oneself or to answer honestly. As Kahneman says, "It takes an active and disciplined mind to raise [them]."[66]

What's missing—logically—from this list of questions is "How much have I lost on this investment already?" Whatever you might have lost is a sunk cost and therefore—at least on paper—an irrelevant issue. But our emotions hinder us here. Our fear of fully recognizing the loss leads us to say, "If I just hang on longer, the market might rebound" (and then I won't regret the decision). Following this type of urge, many people hang on to their losing investments and sell their winning ones—just the opposite of an effective investment strategy.

But wait—there's more. You recall from the chapter on myopic loss aversion that the pain of a loss is bigger than the joy of a similar-sized gain. Because everyone wants the loss and its pain to go away, many investors, following a loss, increase the amount of risk that they take. They are hoping for an outsized gain to more than offset the loss, and, in general, that means taking on more risk. They are "doubling down," as they say in

---

66. *Thinking, Fast and Slow,* p. 344.

Las Vegas, hoping that the higher risk will bail them out of the loss position in which they find themselves.

An interesting example of this type of behavior has been extensively documented in horse-racetrack betting. Typically, most bettors have losses after a few races have been run.[67] In an effort to recoup their losses, bettors place more bets on long shots—horses that are unlikely to win but that will have a large payoff if they do. In turn, overbetting reduces the payoffs, making the "investment" in a long shot even worse.[68]

As always, the first step in countering a bias such as the belief that sunk costs are relevant is awareness. You can ask yourself: Is the money I'm thinking about in fact a sunk cost? Has my behavior changed because of the sunk cost? Once you have contemplated these questions, take a deep breath, calm down, and commit to make a more rational decision. If you have someone with whom you discuss your finances, buy her a copy of this book and ask her to help you identify your particular behavioral biases.[69] You can return the favor at some point.

Opportunity Costs

Now let us return to the football game example to illustrate the importance of a second type of cost: ***opportunity cost***. The opportunity cost of any action is what you give up by taking that action. More precisely, it is the most highly valued of the opportunities that you give up (hence the name). Every action has an opportunity cost. If you spend money on a new house, that's money that can't be spent elsewhere. If you spend four

67. The betting system in the United Kingdom and elsewhere is different, but the logic is still valid.
68. See, for example, Peter Asch, Burton G. Malkiel, and Richard E. Quandt, "Racetrack Betting and Informed Behavior," *Journal of Financial Economics* 10, no. 2 (July 1982): 187–94.
69. Yes, that's a blatant plug to buy more than one copy of this book.

hours at the football game, that's four hours you cannot spend doing anything else—such as washing the car (although that might be a low opportunity cost if you don't consider washing the car much fun). Perhaps it is not surprising that economists are obsessed with costs—they are everywhere (costs, not economists). Note that opportunity cost deals with foregone opportunities, which may or may not mean foregone money.

In the case of the football game, attending the game has an opportunity cost—what else could you do with that time? Within the scenario of good weather and good health, the alternative of sitting at home seems relatively unattractive. The enjoyment of attending the game outweighs the lost opportunity to sit at home. But within the bad-weather-and-poor-health scenario, the opportunity to sit at home is more attractive than attending the game, and you decide to stay home. Attendance at the football game becomes the opportunity cost here, which is quite low given that going to the game wouldn't be much fun.

In terms of your personal finances, I urge you to contemplate the opportunity cost of your time. In particular, if markets are hard to predict and stocks hard to pick (see chapter 4), your time is best spent doing something else. I've often marveled at amateur investors who spend their weekends looking for the next "home run" stock. If asked, they may say that there is no cost to their market research as they are doing it with their "free time," but that is not true—what else might they be doing with that time? Starting a new business? Working a part-time job? Spending time with their families? Every action has an opportunity cost, but often we don't realize it. That's one reason why economists are so focused on the topic.

Marginal Costs

We now turn to our third and last cost: ***marginal cost***. To a noneconomist, *marginal* has a negative connotation: "He's a marginal tuba player." But to an economist, *marginal* simply means "additional" or "incremental." So when you work an extra hour on Friday, that's a marginal hour. When you eat a second ice-cream cone, it is a marginal cone—marginal, that is, to the first one. Marginal therefore also refers to "one more" of something.

The concept of marginal cost is important to all decision making because good decisions are often made "at the margin." Should you work an hour of overtime? The marginal cost is, in fact, the opportunity cost of that hour: What are you giving up by working that extra hour? What else could you have done with that extra time? The marginal benefit, from a financial viewpoint, is the wage you earn for that extra hour. You don't (or shouldn't) compare working forty-one hours a week (the total) with working zero hours per week: you should compare working forty-one hours a week to working forty hours a week. That's a comparison "at the margin."

Let's consider a thought experiment. Think about your investment portfolio and imagine that it is fully invested in "safe" government bonds. Now imagine changing the asset allocation to add one unit of risk to the portfolio. What do you get for that? Generally, you expect a higher return from a higher level of risk. If the increase in return is enough to more than offset your discomfort with the risk, this marginal adjustment makes sense.

Now imagine adding a second unit of risk. Again, you hope to be rewarded with an even higher return. Is it potentially higher enough to more than offset the discomfort you feel about the increase in risk? If yes, make the adjustment; if no, don't.

Have you noticed? You are now making decisions at the margin—congratulations! Continuing with the thought experiment, at some point you will decide that the (next) marginal increase in return does not compensate for the marginal increase in risk. Time to stop taking on risk: you've arrived at your optimal risk level. The marginal way of thinking has led you to a good decision. And though this thought experiment might strike you as merely theoretical, some financial advisors tease out their clients' risk tolerance using a similar exercise by quizzing them about potential payoffs and the associated risks. And determining your risk tolerance is a hugely practical thing to do.

Now let us return to where we started—sunk costs. When people first learn about sunk costs, they sometimes arrive at a misconception: they believe that a decision resulting in sunk costs should necessarily be abandoned. That's not the case. Consider the earlier scenario in which a healthy you decides to attend the football game on a good weather day. The cost of the ticket was a sunk cost, but you went ahead because it was worth your while. In the alternative scenario (bad weather and poor health), you decided not to go. That's irrelevance in action—the original ticket price played no role in your decision in either scenario. If the presence of sunk costs meant not moving forward, sunk costs would be relevant. They are not.

But here's a subtle point: sunk costs often influence marginal costs, and as we've seen, marginal costs (and benefits) are relevant to good decision making. Consider this example: a new office building in which you are investing takes fourteen months to build. After the thirteenth month, most of the costs associated with this project are sunk. But that doesn't necessarily mean it should be abandoned. The marginal cost (one more month of work) is relatively low, and the marginal benefit (a completed commercial property) is very high. It probably makes sense to finish it. Although the sunk cost has influenced the marginal cost, the sunk cost is irrelevant—better to make a marginal decision, as strange as that might sound.

In sum, resist the call of your emotions and ignore sunk costs, once they are actually sunk. Rev up System 2 instead. Recognize that thinking in terms of marginal costs and benefits results in good decisions. And be aware that all actions have some opportunity cost associated with them, even if it is just the cost of time rather than money. That's why economist Milton Friedman famously said, "There's no such thing as a free lunch," to which I would add, "even if someone else is paying the bill."

CHAPTER 9

THE INFORMATION FIRE HOSE

Drinking Drops from a Deluge

Our brain is constantly bombarded by sensory input; by one estimate, our five senses send nearly eleven million bits of information per second to the brain for processing.[70] But, in fact, the brain can actually only process a tiny fraction of this amount. This experience is akin to trying to drink water from a fire hose—yes, you can get a bit of water down your throat from the experience, but one way or another most of it will end up on the floor.

We deal with this figurative deluge by subconsciously inserting mental filters that determine what information gets processed and what merely passes into our mental ether. These filters are, for the most part, not consciously created. In evolutionary terms, the filters are selected for survival—that is, we

---

70. Source: http://www.britannica.com/EBchecked/topic/287907/information-theory/214958/Physiology.

pay particular attention to information that relates as a threat to our well-being (Is that a lion behind the tree?).

If this description sounds familiar, it should. Cognitive biases can serve as filters, as they cause us to focus on some information while downplaying other data. They are helpful because they let us drink drops from the fire hose, but they can sometimes mislead us. In this chapter, I will alert you to four particularly tricky filters that interfere with good financial decision making, and provide some thoughts about how to minimize their negative effects.

Confirmation Bias

This commonly encountered bias encourages the brain to be more receptive to information that is congruent with our beliefs, while being less receptive to information that challenges our beliefs. There is much discussion of how ***confirmation bias*** operates and why it is so entrenched. Harvard University psychologist Daniel Gilbert has studied this phenomenon extensively; he has shown that the more preoccupied our rational thinking capacity, the more likely we are to believe a nonsensical statement.[71,72] Of course, this does not fully account for confirmation bias but does suggest that it is easier for us to disbelieve statements that are contrary to our existing beliefs simply because we are less likely to subject them to rational analysis.

My own conjecture is that humans hugely value being seen as consistent in their beliefs. After all, don't you tend to

---

71. Daniel T. Gilbert, "How Mental Systems Believe," *American Psychologist* 46, no. 2 (February 1991).
72. Daniel T. Gilbert, Douglas S. Krull, and Patrick S. Malone, "Unbelieving the Unbelievable: Some Problems in the Rejection of False Information," *Journal of Personality and Social Psychology* 59, no. 4 (October 1990): 601–13.

discount the credibility of someone who believes one thing one day and another thing the next day? So once we have an even modestly entrenched belief, we are inclined to filter information in such a way as to support that belief. As Julius Caesar said, "People easily believe that which they want to believe."[73] The idea has been around a long time.

Whatever its underlying causes, confirmation bias has been consistently demonstrated. We can rest assured that it is a real phenomenon. As a vivid example, we see this bias operate extensively in the political arena—rarely do political opponents entertain the notion in a public setting that their own previously avowed beliefs and policy positions might be wrong.

How does this apply to minimizing your foolish corner? In today's environment, there is an enormous amount of financial information being flung at us. There are finance-related shows on television every hour of the day. The Internet provides a seemingly infinite amount of "information" (that's in quotes on purpose) about companies to invest in, stock prices and charts, strategies to make you rich, and hot tips about the Next Great Invention and how to benefit from it. There is a major financial market open almost any time of day, so you can trade anytime you want, with real-time news and information coming to you via your broker's website or on your mobile device.

How do we decide what financial information to pay attention to? Well, we don't necessarily decide consciously, but we do decide. And confirmation bias leads us to pay attention to information that supports our beliefs. For example, if you believe that Rearden Rectifiers Inc. is a good investment, you will downplay an analyst's report that suggests it is overvalued and hence a lousy investment. In essence, you filter out the

73. For Latin buffs, here is the original: *"Libenter homines id quod volunt credunt."*

possible bad news about Rearden Rectifiers and let the positive news through.

Counteracting the confirmation bias is, in principle, easy—be more open to information that might cause you to change your mind. Because of our fear of being inconsistent, we might feel that contrary information is a threat to us. But would you rather be dogmatically consistent or make better decisions? Take some advice from a famous economist who was also a successful investor, John Maynard Keynes: "When the facts change, I change my mind."[74]

Availability Bias

Another filter that we use to screen information is the "availability heuristic"—our tendency to rely on information that is readily recalled. As with confirmation bias, there is a substantial body of research that convincingly documents the existence of the ***availability bias***. Perhaps not surprisingly, many things influence availability; let me give you a quick sampling here.[75]

First, events that happen to us personally—as opposed to strangers—are more available for recall. If I've experienced a large loss on an investment, it will be more memorable than reading that others had the same outcome. If I've been cheated by an investment advisor, this is a more vivid memory than reading about someone else's similar woes. One consequence

---

74. This version is quoted in Gillian Tett's "Ideas adjust to new 'facts' of finance," *Financial Times*, December 26, 2013. Other variations exist, for example, "When my information changes, I alter my conclusions," found at http://www.goodreads.com/quotes. Keynes also is reported to have then asked a listener, "What do you do, sir?" Regardless, the sentiment is the same.
75. If you want more detail, Kahneman devotes a whole chapter (12) to the topic of availability in *Thinking, Fast and Slow.*

of availability is an overestimation of the recurrence of the event. Following a large investment loss, people tend to dial back the risk of their investments.

Second, an event or piece of information that really grabs your attention is more likely to be recalled. If you are a follower of pop culture, you know which celebrities are notorious for bad behavior—the headlines jump off the page. Here again, the implication of the availability of such events is an overestimation of the frequency of the event. Ask a teenager how many hours of Justin Bieber's waking day he misbehaves, and you'll likely get an answer like, "Most of them." This is (almost) certainly not true.

Finally, dramatic events also lead to greater availability. People are less likely to fly following a well-publicized plane crash. An extreme example of this behavior was the great reluctance to fly after 9/11. Similarly, people are more likely to buy insurance *after* a natural disaster, because they overestimate the chance of recurrence. Note that these last two multipliers of availability relate to the media coverage of events. Kahneman states, "[Availability] is largely determined by the extent of coverage in the media."[76]

What can be done to combat the availability bias? As we've seen before, awareness is the key. You can then look for evidence that you are giving too much weight to your most readily recallable information. For example, over the course of your investing history, how many investments have suffered a great loss? You may discover that relatively few have, suggesting that you are giving too much weight to that one bad event you suffered or a small handful of them.

---

76. *Thinking, Fast and Slow*, p. 8.

Recency Bias

The effect of ***recency bias*** was originally documented in the psychological experiments dealing with memorization. Asked to memorize a list of words, most people tend to remember the last words on the list best.[77] Because more recent information is better remembered, it is given a disproportional weight. In turn, this can lead to poor decision making.

Consider the case of a "hot" mutual fund, one whose recent returns have been well above average. An investor under the influence of the recency effect will regard the recent returns as representative, and in his mind he will implicitly expect above-average future returns. Consistent with this narrative, research has repeatedly shown that the flow of new money from clients into mutual funds is related to recent returns. Yet research has also shown that mutual fund outperformance is typically short-lived.

To avoid giving undue weight to recent events, take a "historic" view. In the long run, how has a mutual fund performed? In the long run, how have your investing decisions turned out? Consciously underweight recent events to balance out your natural tendency to overweight them.

Familiarity Bias

Somewhat related to the recency effect is the ***familiarity bias***. As the name suggests, this bias consists of giving disproportionate weight to ideas, information, and events that

77. There is also a "primacy effect," in which people tend to remember the items that are first on the list. Combining the primacy and recency effects, we see that the items in the middle are least likely to be remembered. Because the flow of financial information has no clear beginning, I focus on the recency effect here.

are familiar. Note that recent events are often familiar; hence, there is overlap between these two biases.

The familiarity bias has at least two implications for investing. First, many people own stock in the company they work for. Needless to say, this is not the way to create a well-diversified portfolio. Your income depends on the viability of the firm, and so does its stock price. When the firm does poorly, you can lose your job as well as your investment. Employees at the Houston energy firm Enron were encouraged to invest heavily in the company's stock, and many did so, to their great regret. Other examples, such as Lehman Brothers, abound.

Second, the familiarity bias leads people to invest in companies only from their home country. A full discussion of international diversification is beyond the scope of this book, but not putting all your eggs in one country's basket makes sense, doesn't it? The benefits of international diversification have been thoroughly documented.

All these biases—confirmation, availability, recency, and familiarity—can easily lead to poor decisions. Without conscious effort on your part to counter these tendencies, poor decisions are inevitable. However, being aware of the biases and acting to offset their influence will lead you to improved, more rational decisions.

Compounding the problems arising from these four filters, and others, is the issue that the flow of financial information is selective. Ever see one of those late-night infomercials that try to sell you a ten-part series of lectures on how to invest in real estate with no money down? Ever see testimony from someone who bought that course who then also went bankrupt by taking those lessons to heart? Of course not. Does that mean that nobody ever went bankrupt investing in real estate with no money down? Of course not. Those cases just don't get much, if any, attention, and probably they are purposefully buried.

Generally, success stories are reported with greater frequency than failure stories. How many magazine articles have appeared in the past twelve months about the success and genius of Warren Buffett? Many. How many articles have appeared about investors who have tried to follow his investing philosophy and lost money? To my knowledge, none. Does that mean that nobody has lost money trying to mimic Warren Buffett? Think again. What you're observing is a selective flow of information that is not representative of the full spectrum of financial reality.

By the way, the selectivity of the information highway certainly is not limited to the financial world. Consider ten hypothetical studies that examine the effectiveness of a medication. One shows that the medicine is efficient, nine show that it is not: therefore, most of the evidence suggests a lack of efficiency. But which study do you suppose is more likely to get published—and to attract publicity? This phenomenon is wonderfully summarized in the title of a famous article, "Why Most Published Research Findings Are False."[78]

Having said that, I'd like to add one more tool to your behavioral finance toolbox: the premortem. It's an excellent sledgehammer for busting up a wide range of biases, including those related to information overload. The premortem was first developed by the psychologist Gary Klein,[79] though it certainly had existed for centuries in many guises. The topic here is thinking about the future: for example, how your portfolio might perform over the next year, or between now and your planned retirement date.

It is well known that humans, even highly paid ones with fancy degrees, are not good at forecasting the financial future.

---

78. John P. A. Ioannidis, *PLoS Medicine* 2, no. 5 (August 2005).
79. Gary Klein, "Performing a Project Premortem," *Harvard Business Review*, September 2007. A detailed description of the article can be found at http://hbr.org/2007/09/performing-a-project-premortem.

You may have heard the saying "Economic forecasters exist to make fortune-tellers look good." There is enough truth in that statement to provide both comedy and tragedy.

Although we cannot reliably forecast what *will* happen, it is possible for us to think constructively about what *could* happen. This is where the premortem comes in. Before you undertake an important project, mentally picture that, say, a year from now, the project has turned out to be a disaster. Write out what went wrong, in as much detail as you can stand—this is your premortem.[80] The premortem can serve as a road map to a more effective undertaking of the project, in part by helping you take steps to reduce the negative consequences of the worst imagined outcome or to reduce the chances of it happening.

For example, suppose your "project" is your retirement portfolio. A premortem might include something like this: "At the moment, my portfolio is heavily invested in my company's stock. My premortem: a year from now, my company is bankrupt and my stock worthless." This imagined worst case might lead you to restructure your portfolio by selling off some of your company's stock and buying a well-diversified, low-expense mutual fund or exchange-traded fund.

A premortem will not only lead to better decision making but also make you healthier psychologically. Fabled writer and lecturer Dale Carnegie used to say that once you've identified the worst case and realized that you can live through it, you can stop worrying about it and devote your energies to preventing it from happening. I can vouch personally from painful experience that this is a much better approach to life than burying your head in the sand and denying the possibility that anything could possibly go wrong—a method favored by ostriches and overconfident CEOs. When you are truly

80. If you describe all the outcomes that might occur, you are creating a "scenario analysis." The premortem focuses just on the worst possible outcome.

prepared for anything bad that could happen, you maximize your chances of good things happening.

CHAPTER 10

OK, I'VE GOT IT—WHAT NEXT?

Check Out the List

If you've made it this far, you probably agree that, yeah, there is something to all this behavioral finance stuff. Intuitively we're aware that our rational mind isn't always steering the ship when making important financial decisions. Instead, emotional rumblings below deck often take over. What I find particularly helpful about behavioral finance, plus some of the other lessons mentioned herein about human behavior, is that researchers have put labels on these rumblings and dissected them in thoughtful ways, allowing us to better see what they are. In other words, the implicit has been made explicit.

Still, there is a lot to remember. Just to help you out a bit, I have listed all the behavioral biases and mind traps discussed in this book in a handy summary table that follows this chapter. Alongside each bias I have summarized the "remedy" proposed.

You can use this list in several ways. First, you could ask yourself the question, "Which one of these biases/issues most affects me?" At this point, you should have a pretty good idea about that. Perhaps there are three or four that you know have been particularly problematic for you. For many people, including myself, myopic loss aversion has been right at the top of the heap, or close to it. Determine to work on using the remedies for these thorny biases; then down the road, when you view the list again, see whether you feel you have made progress. If not, you may need to delve deeper into the particular issues (see further reading below).

Second, you can refer to this list as needed, when you sense a bias starting to creep into your decision making—or when you see one surfacing in someone close to you. Then you could recall the remedy and apply it yourself or encourage someone else to do so.

Third, you could also make a commitment to view this list at specific times throughout the year. If you usually review your portfolio, say, four times a year, then it would be a great idea to start off that review with a scan of this list. If you view your portfolio less frequently, I would still recommend looking over this list at regular intervals over the year. Either way, it would be helpful to see what kind of progress—or lack of it—has been made since you last reviewed the list.

For a deeper dive into some items, I can suggest some further reading. Here are some books that I have found particularly helpful. They are all fairly recent, but some are already classics in the field:

- *Predictably Irrational: The Hidden Forces That Shape Our Decisions* by Dan Ariely (New York: HarperCollins Publishers, 2008). This is a fascinating account of one academic's conversion to the subject of behavioral finance, and a walk through much of his sometimes quirky but always thought-provoking research. There are many lessons to be learned here.

- *Influence: The Psychology of Persuasion* by Robert B. Cialdini (New York: Harper Business, 2006—revised edition). This is a classic work for marketing professionals everywhere but also for anyone who wants to better understand how mind traps work. An especially compelling discussion of social influences, including the herd instinct, on our behavior.
- *Thinking, Fast and Slow* by Daniel Kahneman (New York: Farrar, Straus and Giroux, 2011). Kahneman is the godfather of behavioral finance and still going strong in his eighties. This is his magnum opus for the masses, and it contains a lifetime of exploration and research into how humans actually behave—not how they think they behave.
- *Misbehaving: The Making of Behavioral Economics* by Richard H. Thaler (New York: W. W. Norton & Company, 2015). An easily accessible history of behavioral finance from one of its guiding lights that focuses on Thaler's battles to bring recognition to this important new area of academic study. Along the way he nicely explains some of the more significant lessons learned, putting them into useful context. Fascinating and inspiring, and especially important for anyone interested in the intersection—and combat zone—between economics and psychology.
- *Stumbling on Happiness* by Daniel Gilbert (New York: Vintage Books, 2007). One of my favorite books, as it explores how humans can be happy, which is certainly one of the primary goals of the behavioral finance experts. Gilbert provides his own prescription, and there is much attention paid to the issues raised in chapter 1: "Compared to What?"
- *Learned Optimism: How to Change Your Mind and Your Life* by Martin E. P. Seligman (New York: Vin-

> tage Books, 2006). Written by one of the pioneers of the "positive psychology" movement, the book shows why optimism improves quality of life, and provides specific guidance about ways in which to increase your optimism level.

Lastly, good luck in your journey. I hope it will be as bias-free as you can make it and that you successfully avoid spending any time lingering in that foolish corner of the mind.

SUMMARY OF BEHAVIORAL BIASES AND OTHER MIND TRAPS

BIAS / MIND TRAP	CHAPTER	PAGE	WHAT IT IS
hedonic adaptation	1: Compared to What?	8	the exciting becomes ordinary; what once excited you becomes banal, even boring
hedonic treadmill	1: Compared to What?	9	seeking new excitement after the old excitement becomes ordinary (see hedonic adaptation)—running after an ever-moving target without actually increasing your long-term happiness
money illusion	2: Money Illusion	14	confusing the number of dollars in your wallet or purse with what those dollars can actually buy
individual purchasing power	2: Money Illusion	19	your personal cost of living; differs from person to person depending on what you spend your money on
odd-even pricing	2: Money Illusion	19	Example: $9.99 instead of $10.00
pretax pricing	2: Money Illusion	20	quoted price excludes taxes
currency adjustment	2: Money Illusion	21	foreign currencies can seem like Monopoly money, not real
credit cards vs. cash	2: Money Illusion	22	easier to spend when using a credit card

REMEDIES / SUGGESTIONS

- don't think of your life in relative terms
- diminish effects of relative thinking by considering the questions "Compared to what?" and "Compared to whom?"
- use negative visualization

- increase awareness
- choose your comparison group carefully—consider comparisons with those far less well-off, as well as historical comparisons
- use negative visualization

- increase awareness
- use calculations to find real costs

- become aware of the true purchasing power of your income

- round numbers to combat marketing spin; don't focus on the 9—think of it as a 10

- increase awareness of the total expenditure with tax

- increase awareness of foreign exchange rates and how to convert to your home currency
- use calculations to find real costs

- increase awareness
- curb credit card use

BIAS / MIND TRAP	CHAPTER	PAGE	WHAT IT IS
myopic loss aversion	3: Myopic Loss Aversion	25	making irrational, short-term decisions in response to losses because they are so painful (see prospect theory)
prospect theory	3: Myopic Loss Aversion	25	the pain of a loss exceeds the pleasure we get from a gain of the same magnitude
pattern recognition	4: The Randomness Trap	33	attempting to find patterns when, in fact, patterns in financial markets are rare
hot-hand phenomenon	4: The Randomness Trap	37	the belief that streaks (wins, losses) will continue longer than they actually do
herd behavior	5: Herd on the Street—and in the Office	41	going with the crowd
affect bias	5: Herd on the Street—and in the Office	43	largely irrelevant characteristics of an asset affect our perception of it
overconfidence	6: Cheery-O's—Optimism and Overconfidence	52	confidence beyond what is justified by the facts
optimism	6: Cheery-O's—Optimism and Overconfidence	52	anticipating positive outcomes; one way to become more satisfied
level of savings	7: Tying Yourself to the Mast	63	failure to save enough, if at all

REMEDIES / SUGGESTIONS

- come up with and be consistent about a strategy for viewing your portfolio (probably best done quarterly), trading, and rebalancing (probably best done annually)
- give yourself a cooling-off period before making purchases

- think calmly about gains and losses, trying to remove the emotional element of your reaction to a gain or loss

- avoid looking for patterns
- be aware when you are explaining the success of an investment, or someone else is explaining theirs, of whether the narrative is based on a pattern that really isn't a pattern

- increase awareness

- increase confidence in your own ability to think independently; take pride in being a bit of a maverick

- increase awareness (e.g., does the lighting of the store make you feel more like buying?)
- use discomfort as a warning sign
- analyze for yourself (rather than letting the herd do it for you)
- consider a wide range of viewpoints
- find a devil's advocate

- challenge your beliefs, consider alternative explanations and scenarios, and ask others for different perspectives

- increase optimism using techniques from *Learned Optimism*, but continue to see the value of pessimism
- be humble and agnostic about what you think you know
- uncertainty is omnipresent; get comfortable with this idea

- realize that saving itself is crucial (so focus on this first and foremost)
- get into the habit of saving—early in life, if possible

BIAS / MIND TRAP	CHAPTER	PAGE	WHAT IT IS
sense of inadequacy	7: Tying Yourself to the Mast	63	head in the sand about the importance of saving
evolutionary myopia	7: Tying Yourself to the Mast	66	when sacrifices are short-term and benefits are long-term, it is tough to do the right thing
framing	7: Tying Yourself to the Mast	72	your perspective or point of view on an issue can influence your decision—do you view saving as lost consumption or an investment in the future?
sunk cost	8: Thinking That Will Weigh You Down	78	an expenditure of time, money, and energy that cannot be retrieved; water under the bridge, so to speak
opportunity cost	8: Thinking That Will Weigh You Down	81	what you are giving up to undertake a particular action (e.g., time spent at work is time not spent with family and friends)
marginal cost	8: Thinking That Will Weigh You Down	83	the cost of doing one more thing (e.g., buying one more doughnut after having already bought a dozen)

REMEDIES / SUGGESTIONS

- face up to reality and create a realistic, implementable plan for saving for retirement

- use payroll deduction for savings
- start retirement savings early in life
- use the Save More Tomorrow plan and institute a penalty for yourself for not complying, such as donating to a cause you oppose
- consider making a public commitment
- think about saving for others (e.g., your spouse, partner, or children)
- think about saving for your future self; have a conversation with your future self, and let him or her thank you for saving now; try "age-progression" software

- reframe the consequences of spending; consider the cost of time needed to make a purchase and other opportunity costs
- pay in cash
- consider your retirement plan as a very individual case
- review your retirement plan once a year

- ask yourself if the money you're thinking about is in fact a sunk cost; ask whether your behavior has changed because of the sunk cost
- if you have someone with whom you discuss your finances, buy them a copy of this book and ask them to help you identify your particular behavioral biases (in regard to sunk costs)

- consider opportunity costs (e.g., of the time you might spend choosing and managing your investments), and determine to what degree these costs are worthwhile

- think "marginally" about risk and other similar factors in order to make more-rational decisions

BIAS / MIND TRAP	CHAPTER	PAGE	WHAT IT IS
confirmation bias	9: The Information Fire Hose	88	greater acceptance of information that supports (confirms) your beliefs; occasionally even seeking out such information
availability bias	9: The Information Fire Hose	90	evidence that is easily available—or easy to recall—is given disproportionate weight
recency bias	9: The Information Fire Hose	92	evidence that is more recent is given disproportionate weight
familiarity bias	9: The Information Fire Hose	92	evidence that is more familiar is given disproportionate weight

REMEDIES / SUGGESTIONS

- be more open to information that might change your mind; read points of view that differ from your own

- raise awareness (e.g., ask yourself if you are giving too much weight to your most readily recallable information, then use the answers to make more-rational decisions)

- take the historic view: try consciously underweighting recent events to counter your tendency to overweight them

- make sure you don't have all your eggs in one (familiar) basket

ACKNOWLEDGMENTS

Many thanks to Charles Parker, former professor at Colorado College, and in memoriam to Elizabeth A. Geiser, founder of the Publishing Institute at the University of Denver. Both were exceedingly helpful during the early development of this book. Also many thanks to entrepreneur extraordinaire Rebecca Brei for her wise edits and counsel.

ABOUT THE AUTHORS

John Howe, PhD, CFA®, is chair of the Department of Finance at the University of Missouri, where he has taught finance for more than two decades and has received awards for excellence in teaching. His writings on banking, corporate finance, corporate governance, and behavioral finance have been published extensively in major finance and accounting journals. Howe has also taught at the University of Cambridge and has trained investment professionals in Zurich at one of Switzerland's largest banks. He is a long-standing member of the editorial board of the *CFA Digest,* the primary publication of the Chartered Financial Analyst Institute.

Robb Corrigan is a London-based communications, marketing, and branding consultant, focusing on the asset-management industry. He has nearly two decades of experience working at major financial firms and start-ups in the United States and Europe, including serving as global head of corporate communications for Barclays Global Investors, global head of communications for Man Group, and head of marketing communications in Europe, the Middle East, and Africa for Merrill Lynch.

Made in United States
North Haven, CT
15 November 2022